THE GRAD'S GUIDE TO

CHOOSING WELL

THE GRAD'S GUIDE TO

CHOOSING WELL

WISDOM FOR LIFE ON YOUR OWN

With thanks to the college students from the Campus Crusade for Christ group at U-W Oshkosh in Oshkosh, Wisconsin, and the students from visiting teacher Linda Taylor's special May term class at Houghton College, Houghton, New York. They took time to write encouraging comments to those coming a few steps behind them in life.

This book is a gift to:

Rachel white

From:

Uncle Roonnie & Aunt Lisa

On this day:

June 7, 2010 (graduation)

I'M PROUD OF YOU

Who you are and what you have accomplished.

I'M GLAD FOR YOU

Your successes and open doors.

And I'm thankful for this ending wrapped around an

exciting beginning for your life.

NavPress

NavPress is the publishing ministry of The Navigators, an international Christian organization and leader in personal spiritual development. NavPress is committed to helping people grow spiritually and enjoy lives of meaning and hope through personal and group resources that are biblically rooted, culturally relevant, and highly practical.

For a free catalog go to www.NavPress.com
or call 1.800.366.7788 in the United States or 1.800.839.4769 in Canada.

ISBN-13: 978-1-60006-921-5

Cover design by studiogearbox.com
Cover image by Veer

Produced with the assistance of The Livingstone Corporation (www .LivingstoneCorp.com). Project staff included writer Neil Wilson.

Unless otherwise identified, all Scripture quotations in this publication are taken from *THE MESSAGE* (MSG). Copyright © 1993, 1994, 1995, 1996, 2000, 2001, 2002. Used by permission of NavPress Publishing Group. Other versions used include: The Holy Bible, English Standard Version (ESV), copyright © 2001 by Crossway Bibles, a division of Good News Publishers. Used by permission. All rights reserved; and the King James Version (KJV).

Printed in the United States of America

1 2 3 4 5 6 7 8 / 14 13 12 11 10

CONTENTS

INTRODUCTION

Someone wants to help you make wise choices. That's why he or she gave you this book. That person knows you're going to be on your own soon and hopes you'll take along some lessons in making choices that others have learned the hard way ahead of you. He or she knows you're going to make some mistakes along the way but hopes you'll consider that some mistakes really aren't worth making. You can tell that person thanks, but the best way to show your gratitude is to read these pages and put what you learn into practice.

In the meantime, congratulations! Graduating from high school is often the first major achievement in a person's life. Whatever your parents may say, this time has arrived too quickly. Yesterday you were taking your first stumbling steps, and today you are walking across the stage to receive your diploma. It all happened in the blink of an eye, even though it might have felt as if this day would never come. Freedom and life on your own are on the horizon.

On my first day of college, I ended up in the student commons, hanging out between classes with several dozen other students. A girl at the table where I was seated proceeded to chain-smoke her way through a pack of cigarettes. (A few years later, the place became a smoke-free zone.) I finally could resist no longer and tossed her a question through the fog that surrounded her: "Do you really like to smoke that much?"

"Actually," she said, "I'm not really a smoker. This is just the first time no one is here to tell me to stop, so I won't." Then she started coughing and I left.

For many of us, freedom does seem like the opportunity to finally do anything we want to do. As we move away from home, we'll meet many people who are trying to live out their belief that freedom means not having anyone tell them to stop, so they don't.

But a person who is developing wisdom sees that when our idea of freedom means doing anything we want to do, it quickly turns into slavery. We become trapped in our wants of the moment rather than living above our wants and desires. Wisdom doesn't ignore wants and desires, but wisdom doesn't let wants and desires have the last word or veto power. Wisdom makes decisions that direct feelings to "Deal with this!"

You are making a wise choice at this moment. You have opened a book about making wise choices. That's a start. Lots of people don't get that far. They say they don't want to make stupid mistakes and screw up their lives, but too often they never actually think about what goes into a good decision. They can't answer the question "What makes a wise choice?" You now have an opportunity to work out your answer to that question.

The Grad's Guide to Choosing Well will start with a story of someone who illustrates that it's never too late to learn true wisdom. Then we will look at the Choice Matrix, the basic idea that there are tools we can use to make good decisions and live wisely. After we understand the Choice Matrix, we will apply it to a number of life situations that you may face in the future and think about how it can be used to make decisions in "everything we do" and "everywhere we go" (see Proverbs 3:5-6).

The apostle Paul pointed to a wise way of living when he told his friends in the church at Ephesus,

> *Watch your step. Use your head. Make the most of every chance you get. These are desperate times!*
> *Don't live carelessly, unthinkingly. Make sure you understand what the Master wants. (Ephesians 5:15-17)*

ZAC'S STORY: A FUNNY THING
HAPPENED ON THE WAY TO WISDOM

Zac and I met after high school, but over time I realized that our growing-up years had a lot in common. It wasn't that we were born in the same place or lived in the same neighborhood or even faced the same situations, but still, the more I thought about Zac's early years, the more I knew we were very much alike.

Zac was short. We've all got that one thing we think is really obvious about us that really bothers us about ourselves, and for Zac it was his height. It wasn't just his imagination—he really was short. He started out short. You know how they measure babies when they're born? Well, the nurse looked at Zac and said, "Hmmm. What a short baby!"

For Zac there were other reminders. His parents gave him

a longer name but always called him Zac. You know how your mother says your name when she's upset with you? She says your whole name deliberately, and if she's really mad she adds your middle and last names too? Well, Zac's parents didn't do that. They always said "Zac." And when they were angry, they just said, "ZAAAAC!"

Being small can be hard when you start going to school. For one thing, you get overlooked. In Zac's case, this was serious. The first day of class, he found a desk to sit at and then had to protest when a couple other people tried to sit on top of him because they didn't notice him there. "Hey! Someone's already in this chair!"

Zac's growth spurt never arrived. When it came to athletics, some coaches just ignored him, while others treated him like a lawsuit ready to happen. He went out for football, but they couldn't find equipment small enough to fit him. The coach admitted he was relieved because he didn't want to have to pry Zac out from between someone else's cleats if he got stepped on. Actually, there were quite a few jokes that used Zac's size for the punch line. Zac never laughed.

So Zac was relegated to being manager/water boy for every team he tried to join. After a while, he stopped trying to work on his athletic skills and concentrated instead on his resentments. Once he shifted his attention, he discovered he was very good at math. He knew how to juggle figures with the best of them. His grades were good and he began to think about what he might do for a job in the future.

Where does someone work who gets overlooked by people,

carries some resentments about past treatment, but isn't really big enough to get even with people for the way they've treated him? Zac soon found the perfect job: He went to work for the IRS.

Now, in Zac's day, IRS stood for the Israeli Revenue Service. And the system worked a little different than the IRS we are familiar with today. In Zac's time, IRS agents made their wages by overcharging their clients on taxes for the Roman Empire. Zac had very simple business cards made, and he took pride in the fact that his were just a little bigger than standard. On his he had a scribe write, "Zacchaeus, Tax Collector."

For Zac, this arrangement was perfect. People brought in their W-2 forms and Zac worked his magic. He never found a deduction he couldn't deny, he had a nose for undeclared income, and he created fees and surcharges out of thin air. He didn't care that his clients resented the size of their tax bill. He was getting even (and then some). He was a skillful tax collector. Before long, Zacchaeus was a wealthy man—lonely and despised, but rich. He lived in a fine house in Jericho and was feared and hated by his neighbors. He was well on his way to living unhappily ever after.

Along the way, however, Zac developed an interesting quirk. He spent a lot of time by himself, but he observed others carefully. He was fascinated by unusual people. His line of work made everyone so ordinary that he was instantly drawn to figuring out people who lived outside the stereotypes. He noticed freaks, partly because he considered himself one.

So it was probably inevitable that when Zac started hearing

about a healer/teacher named Jesus, he became curious. The stories he heard about Jesus puzzled him. Here was a guy who went around doing good yet was resented by a lot of people. Zac chuckled and thought, *I know why people resent me. I wonder why Jesus is so hated?*

One busy day, Zac heard that Jesus was going to be passing through Jericho, and he made a note to watch out for the traveling show. But he got a little occupied in his work, and by the time he heard the commotion of people gathering on Main Street, he realized he might be too late to catch a glimpse of Jesus.

The last thing a short person wants to do is show up late for a parade. When Zac left his office and approached the main road through town, all he could see was an endless row of backsides as far as he could look either way. Many who made up the solid wall of humanity in front of him at that moment were his disgruntled clients. There was no way they were going to step aside to let the "short tax guy" get a look.

The excited roar of the crowd told Zac that Jesus was approaching. He started to panic. Then he noticed a sycamore tree close by that stood behind the crowd but overhung the road. He rushed over and started to climb up. It was one of those rare times when his size worked to his advantage, because the branch didn't even crack as he crawled out over the crowd and hung on for dear life.

About the time Zac reached his perch, Jesus came walking along, surrounded by his disciples. He stopped under the tree and looked up at the strange fruit hanging there. Jesus' action was so sudden that the noise got quiet in anticipation. People's eyes gradually shifted upward to see what Jesus was looking at. In the momentary stillness, Jesus said, "Hey, Zacchaeus! Why don't you climb down—carefully! I'd like to spend the afternoon at your house."

Zac was so surprised, he almost fell out of the tree. As he hurried down, he heard the roar of surprise and anger from the crowd. People were not happy about Jesus' choice of homes to visit. Resentments toward Zac were almost instantly directed toward Jesus. The refrain he heard several times was "You can't go to *his* house!"

Meanwhile, Zac's heart was in overdrive, reacting from the adrenaline of exercise and excitement. He wondered how on earth Jesus knew his name. And he had a hard time not agreeing with the crowd—why would Jesus want to come to *his* house? He couldn't get over the sudden strange feeling of being noticed.

Zac never told me exactly what Jesus said that afternoon *good* or even what he served the sudden crowd who showed up at his *example* house, but Zac never tired of telling how the afternoon ended. *of* *acceptance* His feelings of being noticed gradually changed into feelings of being accepted for the first time in his life. As Jesus was leaving, Zac knew he didn't want to let this amazing person walk out of his life without making a commitment. The fact that even though Jesus knew his name and (as it turns out) everything about him but still wanted to spend time with him gave Zac a whole new perspective. His priorities got turned upside down. As the New Testament puts it, Zacchaeus said, "Master, I give away half my income to the poor — and if I'm caught cheating, I pay four times the damages" (Luke 19:8). Zac became the kind of person who stopped thinking about what he was going to get out of a situation and started thinking about how he would influence a situation for good. Zacchaeus got a good dose of wisdom that day with Jesus.

As for Jesus, his comment was, "Today is salvation day in this home! Here he is: Zacchaeus, son of Abraham! For the Son of Man came to find and restore the lost" (verses 9-10). Zac came away with a renewed identity and a new life to go with it.

Funny things happen on the way to wisdom. If you want a full, interesting, satisfying, and godly life, make sure you pursue wisdom. And pay attention! You might even find yourself hanging around in a strange place when wisdom comes along. Be ready to go with wisdom anytime it shows up.

THE CHOICE MATRIX

Trust God from the bottom of your heart;
don't try to figure out everything on your own.
Listen for God's voice in everything you do, everywhere you go;
he's the one who will keep you on track.

PROVERBS 3:5-6

The title of this book tells you that we're going to discuss every decision you will ever make — well, more or less. We are not going to *list* all those decisions. We don't have enough pages here to look at the details of the decisions you've already made today, much less a lifetime of choices. And we're not going to discuss every life decision individually. But we are going to talk about what all decisions have in common. And we're going to use some categories of choices you are sure to face. If this book is going to serve as your guide to choosing well, it will have to give you a reliable and true way to make decisions.

One of the first things the Bible tells us, after it describes the sequence of God's creation, is that God decided to make us in his image. The way Genesis 1:27 sums it up,

> *God created human beings;*
> *   he created them godlike,*
> *Reflecting God's nature.*
> *   He created them male and female.*

God is not a big version of us; we are a very simple version of God's characteristics. We think, we communicate, and we create. We also make choices. We can consider a number of alternatives and decide on one course of action. We can look at a menu, place an order, and usually tell someone exactly why we ordered grilled liver and onions (I'll let you explain that!).

A few thousand years later, humans beings, practicing their God-imaging capacities, invented computers. We did this within the limitations of not being God but, in some ways, "godlike." So no one stood in a lab one day and announced, "Let there be computers!" And there wasn't a sudden flash, followed by rows of desktop and laptop machines lined up on the counters, rapidly booting up for action, although that would have been impressive. Unlike God's creation, our creation of computers evolved and continues to do so. Unlike God's creation, our creations can always be improved. But one interesting note about the way we created computers is that we, in a sense, made them in *our image*. Computers are mechanical choice machines. They are programmed to make rapid decisions, and their speed seems to increase every day.

One of the terms that come up frequently in discussing computers is *processing*. A computer receives data and processes it according to the way the machine has been programmed. If we input data from a program that our computer doesn't have, it can't process the information. There's nothing quite like trying to open a document with a crucial assignment over which we have labored for days only to discover that the laptop we're using can't read that file and our carefully constructed sentences are now odd-looking symbols that we know our teacher won't be able to read.

Like computers, we are continuously processing information. In the moments it has taken you to read this far, your mind has darted in various directions, supplying images, memories, examples, and questions, all part of your processing nature. But you are not a computer. You are a unique, priceless, and amazing creation of God. You do bear his image.

A long time ago, someone who was overwhelmed with the thought that he was actually designed personally by God wrote these thoughts:

> *You shaped me first inside, then out;*
> *   you formed me in my mother's womb.*
> *I thank you, High God—you're breathtaking!*
> *   Body and soul, I am marvelously made!*

I worship in adoration — what a creation!
You know me inside and out,
*   you know every bone in my body;*
You know exactly how I was made, bit by bit,
*   how I was sculpted from nothing into something.*
Like an open book, you watched me grow from conception
*   to birth;*
*   all the stages of my life were spread out before you,*
The days of my life all prepared
*   before I'd even lived one day. (Psalm 139:13-16)*

David, the writer, understood that we are neither products of a random biological assembly line nor the results of accidental chemical actions. We are "marvelously made!"

Part of our basic operating system could be called COS (Choice Operating System). Life is about choices, and we were designed to make choices. One of the "marvelous" aspects of our making is that there are countless choices we make every minute that we don't have to do consciously. Think about how many breaths you have taken since you opened this book. How many times has your heart beat? What would happen if you had to make each of those choices intentionally? (Is it time to breathe again? I'm feeling a little light-headed there, heart; let's pick up the pace!). God preprograms us with a lot of our choices being made in the background, special applications that run constantly from conception to death. Your heart will beat millions of times in your lifetime, and you won't have to decide to make it happen. But there are also countless other decisions that you will consciously make while your heart beats away quietly in your chest. Those decisions are the ones we want to give our attention to in these pages.

At this point, you've probably got some questions:

- What is wisdom?
- What is a wise decision?
- How do I know I've made a good and wise decision even before I see the results?
- If I'm responsible for my decisions, does that mean I have to make them on my own? Where do I get help?
- Does wise living mean mistake-free living? Does wise living mean difficulty-free living? If it doesn't, then why should I pursue wise living?

These are all excellent questions. We will address them here and throughout the book. Because wisdom and wise living are the objectives of this book, let's agree with the way the Bible uses the idea of wisdom and describe it as skillful living. Wisdom involves knowing how things should be done. Practicing wisdom means doing whatever you are doing in life as close as possible to how it should be done. Anything and everything you do in life can be done wisely.

I want to introduce you to a tool you can use in making decisions that will lead you toward wisdom. For consistency with the computer language we've been using, we're going to upload a default program into your thinking that will help you evaluate any decision and steer you toward wise choices. The code for that program, which we will call the Choice Matrix, is found in Proverbs 3:5-6:

> Trust ~~God from the bottom of your~~ heart; *(in the Lord with all thine)*
> ~~don't try to figure out everything on your own~~. *(and lean not unto thine own understanding)*
> ~~Listen for GOD's voice in everything you do, everywhere you go;~~ *(In all thy ways acknowledge Him)*
> ~~he's the one who will keep you on track~~. *(and He shall direct thy paths)*

Note there are four distinct phrases in those verses. Read them again and put parentheses around each specific thought. These four principles, and the consistency with which you use them, will have a great deal to do with your pace in developing wisdom as you live on your own.

#1: Trust ~~God from the bottom of your~~ heart. (verse 5a) *(in the Lord with all thine heart)*

Chances are you've been able to live with an easy faith up until now. You may consider yourself a follower of Jesus, but you probably haven't been challenged with what that means in the way you live. There have been people and systems around you that you didn't have a hard time trusting as you've grown up. That situation is about to change big-time as you move away from home. You won't realize how much structure has been around your life until you leave it behind—being reminded to pick up your room, do your homework, take out the trash. You haven't really had to think, *Now, where's my next meal coming from and how will I pay for it?* You've probably lived with a fair amount of direction, which will now be removed. You will be on your own.

Wisdom appreciates external structures, but what we want to focus on here is wisdom's special emphasis on internal structures. Who are you and who directs your life on the inside? How would anyone in your life know that you "trust God from the bottom of your heart"? Until now, perhaps you haven't really had to trust that deeply. You could get by with trusting God with a corner of your heart. But when you are on your own, you have an opportunity to discover how deep your trust in God really goes. You want it to go all the way to the bottom of your heart.

Matt left home for the Air Force right out of high school. He and his family had a tearful farewell at a bus station, and within twenty-four hours, he found himself in a pitch-black barracks, far from home, surrounded by strangers, questioning what had made him think this was going to be fun. He lay there in military pajamas, feeling his fresh, military haircut and remembering the rude experience of yelling sergeants, confusion, and strange rules. Everything external that reminded him of last week's life was gone. He was suddenly in a new life. He heard guys around him weeping quietly. He realized he wasn't the only one waking up to reality.

Later he told his father, "That first night, I started thinking about how alone I was and how far I was from everyone important to me. Then I realized that God was still with me. I lay there on my cot thinking that the God who had been on the edge of my life for a long time had been willing to come along with me to this new place and wouldn't leave me. It was like a light came on in that dark place. That moment was when I began to understand what trusting God was really about."

West Coast Storytelling You may consider that you have a fairly developed trust in God at this point. What examples can you give of decisions you've made based on that trust? (You might want to take a moment and jot these in the margin of this book while you are thinking of them.) On what occasions have you had to trust God in the face of pressure to trust someone? The point is that feeling like we trust God is not quite the same as actually trusting him in a real situation. One thing you can be sure of is that life on your own will challenge and can grow your trust in God.

Lean not unto thine own understanding
#2: ~~Don't try to figure out everything on your own.~~ (verse 5b)

Being on your own doesn't mean you have to make every decision on your own. Develop a list of people who have proven *dad* trustworthy in your life. These are people who have two charac- *mom* teristics: (1) they won't say anything to you simply because it's *Dennis* *Hannah* what you want to hear (in fact, they often tell you what you *don't* *Mrs. Papall* want to hear), and (2) their lives and their counsel are consistent with each other. Don't overlook your parents and grandparents. You may be able to think of two or three people at church who strike you as insightful people whom you wouldn't mind being like later on in life. Beware of anyone, no matter how wise he or she appears, who encourages you to do something they are not willing to do. This is not to say, of course, that it's a good idea to look for company in doing unwise things.

Because you share similar experiences, friends your own age should not be the primary participants in your circle of counsel. You want to seek advice from those who are older than you and can give you the benefit of their added experiences. If you are faced with a decision in a certain specific area, such as education, talk to several people who have had experience in that area. Your friends probably feel the same way you do about school right now, so they won't be much help in thinking seriously about future education.

The second part of the Choice Matrix requires us to answer this question: Have I talked this decision over with people whose counsel has proven trustworthy? ✓ west Coast

#3: ~~Listen for God's voice in everything you do, everywhere you go.~~ (verse 6a)

In all thy ways acknowledge Him

The first part of the Choice Matrix reminds us to base our lives on God's faithfulness and trustworthiness. He is in control of events beyond our power and understanding. But we need to do more than declare our trust in God and then live our lives without asking for his input. This is where the third part of the Choice Matrix fits.

God wants to speak into our decision making. He does this through his written Word (the Bible). Note these interesting comments on the importance of God's Word:

- "How can a young person live a clean life? By carefully reading the map of your Word" (Psalm 119:9).
- "By your words I can see where I'm going; they throw a beam of light on my dark path" (verse 105).

We meet people all the time who are willing to declare that they believe the Bible is the Word of God but know very little of what's in the Bible. To use the above-mentioned verses, these are people whose map from God is still in their glove compartment and whose light from God they haven't turned on.

God's Word provides direction (map), illumination (light), and resources. The choices we make every day build our lives. The quality of our house-structure has a lot to do with how much we have included what God says in how we build. Jesus ended his Sermon on the Mount by telling a little parable to those who had just listened to him. He told his audience that he knew they were one of two kinds of people — smart carpenters and stupid carpenters. And the difference had to do with wisdom:

The wise man built his house upon the rock & the rains came tumbling down - The house stood firm.

These words I speak to you are not incidental additions to your life, homeowner improvements to your standard of living. They are foundational words, words to build a life on. If you work these words into your life, you are like a smart carpenter who built his house on solid rock. Rain poured down, the river flooded, a tornado hit—but nothing moved that house. It was fixed to the rock.

The foolish man built his house upon the sand & the rains came tumbling down - the house went SPLAT

But if you just use my words in Bible studies and don't work them into your life, you are like a stupid carpenter who built his house on the sandy beach. When a storm rolled in and the waves came up, it collapsed like a house of cards. (Matthew 7:24-27)

The third part of the Choice Matrix requires that we answer this question: How does God's Word speak to this decision I'm about to make? Having godly wisdom means that we can trace the choices we're making back to what God has said.

#4: *He shall direct your paths*
#4: ~~He's the one who will keep you on track.~~ **(verse 6b)**

Usually people don't like to fail. We would prefer not to have our glaring mistakes pointed out to us. Most of us don't get up one day and say, *I'm going out of my way to mess up my life today!* We don't want to think, *You know, I've been making some really good decisions here lately. It's about time to make a bunch of bad ones!* We are not only wired to make choices; we are designed to desire to make good choices.

Wise decision making doesn't mean that we never make mistakes, experience failures, or run into brick walls. <u>Wise people have setbacks, but they keep moving forward</u>. So is it worth it to live wisely? Yes. Missionary E. Stanley Jones often pointed out that the life of a follower of Jesus is never immune from hardship and suffering this side of eternity. But ultimately the life of someone who does not follow Christ is harder. For even when an unbeliever is enjoying various blessings, there is a nagging doubt that the good things of life come from someone but they recognize no one to thank.

The fourth part of the Choice Matrix brings us back to ongoing trust in God. When we work through the three earlier parts of the Choice Matrix and things don't go quite as we expected, we have a trust decision to make. Did we miss some direction or information that created the problem? Or is this a case where <u>God has allowed a different outcome that he will use to bring about a better result later</u>? When we are developing

a wise lifestyle, we can't forget that we live in a fallen world
where difficult things happen. As the Bible puts it, ~~"That's why
we can be so sure that every detail in our lives of love for God
is worked into something good"~~ (Romans 8:28).

[handwritten:] And we know that all things work together for good to them that love God & unto them that are the called according to his purpose

APPLYING THE CHOICE MATRIX

As we work our way through various decision areas you are
facing and will face, we will discover how the Choice Matrix
makes the decision-making process more effective. Special
aspects of parts of the Choice Matrix will also become clearer
to you. But before we turn to those case studies, don't miss an
important underlying character trait that wisdom requires. The
main difference between people who have access to a lot of
wisdom and people who actually live wisely is courage *[handwritten: discretic]*. It takes
courage to live skillfully. It takes courage to pursue excellence.
Deciding to live in harmony with God's design may provoke
ridicule from others, even your friends. But they don't have to
live your life—you do. The Choice Matrix will prove to be a
valuable tool as you seek to live wisely, on your own.

THREE WISDOM MANUALS

You probably already know that even though we call the Bible
a book, it is actually a library. It is God's personal collection
of writings, inspired over centuries and preserved for our use.
The Bible is God's operating manual for the unique creatures
that bear his image. While those of us who intend to live for

God should be familiar with the entire operating manual, let me recommend three "volumes" within the Bible that will apply directly to the development of wisdom in your life. Get to know Psalms, Proverbs, and Ecclesiastes.

Psalms is the song sampler that God uploaded to his Word. Make it a habit to download selections from the Psalms to your mental iPod. Spending time in Psalms will deepen the first part of the Choice Matrix in your life. The book of Psalms works trust into your soul and the lowest parts of your heart.

iPod

Proverbs is filled with wise sound bites. The book has thirty-one chapters, which makes it a no-brainer for a chapter-a-day approach. God has included a wealth of pithy and practical observations about living that will often make you smile and sometimes keep you safe.

Ecclesiastes is the most obviously modern book in the Bible, although it was written hundreds of years before Jesus. It is the journal of a man who not only was wise but also demonstrated that though wisdom apart from God can achieve much, in the end it leads to nothing. Living skillfully apart from God turns out to be living for nothing. The writer of Ecclesiastes shows us that great success in any area is meaningless without the same key factors that make up the Choice Matrix. He summed up his hard-learned lessons in these words:

The last and final word is this:

Fear God.
Do what he tells you.

And that's it. Eventually God will bring everything that we do out into the open and judge it according to its hidden intent, whether it's good or evil. (12:13-14)

TOMORROW, TOMORROW

There's an opportune time to do things, a right time for everything on the earth.

ECCLESIASTES 3:1

In downtown Dallas, Texas, there is a busy restaurant that caters to a mixed and boisterous clientele. The place is crowded day and night. One of the large permanent signs hung outside this restaurant has a way of making you think twice. It looks as though it were hand-painted in a hurry. But the announcement is hard to miss: "Free Food and Drink Tomorrow!"

I walked by that restaurant four days in a row, and the sign never changed. Apparently, every night just before midnight, when the food and drinks are about to be passed out at no charge, the tomorrow that was about to arrive suddenly becomes today, and the waiting starts all over again. They figured out the trick. You can promise a lot of things "tomorrow" if you are actually putting them off indefinitely.

You wouldn't do that, would you? Try these statements on for familiarity:

- I'm going to get my room organized . . . tomorrow.
- I'm going to start working on that paper . . . tomorrow.
- That job I need for summer? I'm going to start looking . . . tomorrow.

Tomorrow may never come, but the future does have a way of sneaking up on you. It disguises itself as today.

When it comes to using the Choice Matrix, which we described in the last chapter, I wasn't sure if the future should be the place to start with our case studies. Perhaps it should be the last thing we talk about. But this book is being written at a time in history when the future as a topic of conversation, thought, and concern has moved to the front of the line. Lots of people who thought their futures were safe and secure have suddenly lost almost everything. Certain things have turned out to be uncertain. People who seemed to have it made had it all taken away from them overnight. We have a whole new understanding of "safe bet."

It's big, it's scary, it's unknown — the future. You are probably experiencing various feelings about your future: anxiety, excitement, anticipation, fear. None of those is wrong. They're your feelings. Wisdom isn't about feelings. Wisdom does something with and about feelings but isn't ruled by them. So whatever feelings you may be having about your future, they are serving to highlight the fact that applying wisdom to the future is important.

Let's take the first section of the Choice Matrix and think about how it deals with the future: **Trust God from the bottom of your heart**. Emotions such as anxiety and excitement are like the carbonated bubbles that rise in your soft drink. These feeling bubbles can make your heart seem as if it's about to explode. But notice that wisdom goes to what's at the bottom of your heart, not what's floating around and popping in the air. Feelings come and go, but wisdom sticks around.

Jesus had a couple of things to say about the future. On one memorable occasion, he spoke about the importance of not worrying (see Matthew 6:25-34). At the end of his comments, he said, "Give your entire attention to what God is doing right now, and don't get worked up about what may or may not happen tomorrow. God will help you deal with whatever hard things come up when the time comes" (verse 34).

Jesus knew that worrying messes up today and doesn't accomplish anything about the future. Part of treating the future wisely is to trust God from the bottom of your heart. This means that no matter what you may be feeling, you choose to deliberately and repeatedly tell God, "I'm trusting you with my future."

Now, beyond praying about trusting God, how do we live wisely when it comes to the future? How do we put trust into practice?

The Bible (primarily the book of Proverbs) contrasts wisdom with foolishness. <u>Every choice we make can be described as a wise choice or a foolish choice.</u> When it comes to the future, we can make several popular choices: Try to ignore it ("Don't bother me with the future"), ridicule it ("The future? What future?"), or worry about it ("There's nothing I can do but sit here depressed and scared"). All of these, in their endless variations, fit into the foolish category. Why? Because these statements all indicate a person being deeply affected by the future but not acknowledging it or doing something about it. Or we can handle the future with wisdom, which basically means we make some definite plans and prepare for the days and years to come but never forget that God has the final say on how things turn out. Plans are important, but wise plans aren't written in stone (although we will soon make the case that a plan really isn't a plan until you write it on paper). Making plans is a much wiser way to use the energy we might otherwise invest in worrying, which accomplishes absolutely nothing.

When people say, "I'm not going to make any plans; I'm just going to trust God," they may be expressing more about personal laziness than about trusting God. The test is how they are living right now. If they are not making any plans for the future and not living intentionally today, then they are wasting the gift of *now* that God has given and they are actually saying that they plan to also waste the gift of *then* if and when it comes.

Think of planning as "creative praying." It's a way of putting your desires before God alongside your desire to live for him. We'll come back to this when we look at part three of the Choice Matrix. For now, it might be good to get your hands on a notebook and start tracking the ways you are using the Choice Matrix to practice wise decision making. You can also use it to journal thoughts you have as you are reading this book. I don't know about you, but I realize I have wasted some great thoughts because I didn't take time to write them down. Later I remember that I had a good idea about a project, but it's gone and I can't remember what that thought even was. When I've written things down in the moment, I've often been amazed when I read my notes later.

In your notebook, create a page for each of the chapters in this book, using it as your own case study when we look at these various areas that benefit when we apply the Choice Matrix. Write down each of the parts of the Matrix, leaving space for your notes and conclusions. You're going to be familiar with these by the end of the book, but here they are again:

#1: Trust ~~God from the bottom of your~~ heart. *[handwritten: in the Lord with all thine]*

#2: ~~Don't try to figure out everything on your own.~~ *[handwritten: Lean not unto thine own understanding]*

#3: ~~Listen for God's voice in everything you do, everywhere you go.~~ *[handwritten: In all thy ways acknowledge Him]*

#4: ~~He's the one who will keep you on track.~~ *[handwritten: And He shall direct thy paths]*

Eventually you might want to tell others what you are doing, but the central part of this entire experience is getting clear on trusting God and what that trust means in living *your* life. Planning, dreaming, and setting goals are the bridge between the today you are living and the tomorrow you are preparing to live. Creating a record of your God-centered planning is an expression of trust because you are telling God, "I'm trusting you enough to keep a record of the way you are and will be faithful in my life."

Creating any kind of a record also means that you are planting the seeds of memories. Decades from now, you can look at this transition notebook and track how your plans unfolded in expected and unexpected ways. People often hesitate to create this kind of record because they have a nagging doubt: "What if things don't turn out the way I hoped?" The question is a good one and should be answered. First, you can be sure things aren't going to turn out exactly as you plan. Life's like that. Second, trusting God from the bottom of your heart means, in part, that you can actually expect to discover that things won't turn out the way you plan because God has something better for you.

Trusting God means he has a free hand to improve on our plans. But when we don't make any plans at all, we'll have little idea of how much God does. *When you aim for nothing you'll hit it everytime!*

#2: Don't try to figure out everything on your own.

You may have already created a life plan for yourself. That's great! Make sure you have it in writing. Here's a way to refine it. Make a list of three or four people who are older than you and whose lives you admire. Ask them if they would be willing to tell you about plans they made early in life and how those plans worked out. Have that conversation with them, and make a note of anything you haven't covered in your plans. You don't have to share your plans with them, but you may decide to do so and get their feedback.

Part of not trying to figure out everything on your own means including in your plan some dreams and ideas that you have no way of knowing how you would achieve. Don't leave things out just because you think they are impossible. Trusting God from the bottom of your heart means you're trusting some-one who is all about the impossible. A teenager named Mary was visited by an angel named Gabriel who not only told her she would give birth to the Son of God but also added, "Nothing, you see, is impossible with God" (Luke 1:37). Don't edit you plans with an "unrealistic" pen. Put some things in your plans that make you laugh because they are outlandish. Remember what Paul told his Ephesian friends: "God can do anything, you know—far more than you could ever imagine or guess or request in your wildest dreams! He does it not by pushing us around but by working within us, his Spirit deeply and gently within us" (Ephesians 3:20).

A young man named Joseph (his story is recorded in Genesis chapters 37–50) had some amazing dreams. He pictured a scene in which he was working in a field with his ten older brothers, gathering bundles of grain. Now, that might not seem all that strange because they were all farm kids. But Joseph told his brothers that something unusual happened with their bundles of grain. "All of a sudden my bundle stood straight up and your bundles circled around it and bowed down to mine" (37:7). Younger brothers don't usually get away with telling their older brothers, "I dreamed that someday I am going to be the boss of you!" Joseph's problem wasn't his dream; it was sharing it with people who couldn't accept it. Joseph had no way of knowing how his dream would come true, and he probably wouldn't have been all that excited if he had known ahead of time what a long and hard road he was going to travel before the dream came true. When it comes to sharing all or part of your plan for the future with others, choose your audience carefully. Tell people who can be trusted with even what might seem like a crazy dream.

If you are talking to someone who is in a career that interests you or doing the kind of work you would eventually like to do, ask him or her, "What were the experiences that prepared you the most for what you are doing now?" Other people's journeys can show you a way you might not have seen on your own.

#3: Listen for God's voice in everything you do, everywhere you go.

Under the heading for this chapter, you read the first verse of Ecclesiastes 3, a well-known passage about time. Realize that there's a time component to every decision you make. Deciding to go to college is a decision to invest four or more years in the first level of education beyond high school. Some careers may require even more schooling. Just thinking about that when you can hardly wait to put the last twelve years behind you can bring on a little headache, but time doesn't care how you feel—it keeps on ticking.

Ecclesiastes 3:1-15 offers some amazing thoughts on the nature of God's gift of time to us. Among other things, it tells us to remember that there's a right time for at least twenty-eight different life moments or efforts. And those are just samples. We'll come back to those "times" later on when we look at how we use time wisely, but for now we need to think about God's purpose behind all that he gives to us in life and time. Verse 14 says, "I've also concluded that whatever God does, that's the way it's going to be, always. No addition, no subtraction. God's done it and that's it. That's so we'll quit asking questions and simply worship in holy fear." Now, if you read much of Ecclesiastes, you will see that it is full of questions. The point of verse 14 isn't to keep us from asking *any* questions; the point is to make sure that nothing, not even our questions, keeps us from worshipping God in holy fear.

What is holy fear? Holy fear is the right kind of fear. It's a fear that fits a particular situation. If you're walking along a sunny path in the mountains and almost step off a sudden drop-off of several thousand feet, a jolt of cautious and preserving fear fills you. The unexpected exposure puts you into survival hyperdrive. If you were told that in ten minutes you will have to deliver a speech to a large audience, you would probably begin to feel some symptoms of crowd exposure: weak knees, queasy stomach, dry mouth. Stage fright is an almost universal fear. It's natural and right for that situation as long as it doesn't become the focus but instead becomes part of the energy that makes you do your best.

Holy fear is what happens when we are exposed to God and know we're exposed. It's that deepest, humblest, and purest of all fears when we realize that we live in God's presence and the only reason we are still breathing, thinking, and walking around is because he wants it that way. Holy fear is the right fear to have about God. It's not terror but awe. Ecclesiastes 3 tells us that no matter which of the amazing variety of "times" we are passing through, God is there. And not just "there" but also speaking, so our continual invitation is to "listen for GOD's voice in everything [we] do, everywhere [we] go." The more we know of God's Word, the more we actually hear him speaking to us as we go through our days.

#4: He's the one who will keep you on track.

We can make plans and use them to orient our days. But we must also keep placing our plans and our futures in God's hands. "We plan the way we want to live, but only GOD makes us able to live it" (Proverbs 16:9). A quiet sense of confidence saturates people's lives when they aren't depending on themselves to make it all happen. We may not be able to control tomorrow, but we can plan, prepare, and then take tomorrow as it comes. Experience will teach you that a prepared person is able to be more flexible than a person who goes into each day without any forethought. A person who trusts God really can say, "I may not know what the future holds, but I know who holds the future."

WISE BITES

"Be ready for a different world. It will be completely different than what you are used to. Many nights without much sleep, and drama that can really crush you emotionally."

"The future never runs out of potential. No matter what mistakes you make, there are always second chances. The key is to make the best of your circumstances."

"You don't have to agonize over 'the right way' because God isn't cruel and he's not hiding it from you. If you are seeking God, you're already on the right path, you want what he wants for you, and he plans to give you the desires of your heart."

SURVIVING A SEX-SATURATED WILDERNESS

**God, make a fresh start in me,
shape a Genesis week from the chaos of my life.**

PSALM 51:10

I hadn't really planned to visit the local high school that day, but when I saw the topic for the all-school assembly, I decided to stick around. The sign said, "Today — Assembly on Abstinence." Frankly, I was amazed. This was a public school. When I talked to the principal, I discovered that a rash of pregnancies among his students had been so troubling to him that he had accepted the offer from a group willing to make a sexual abstinence presentation to the school. I complimented him on his courage. Then I asked for permission to observe.

An older gentleman was the presenter, and the students were restless from the start. The speaker based his remarks on good facts, and it was clear that he was passionate about his subject, but the kids were inattentive. His well-meaning points emphasized the dangers of sex and the practical side of virginity until marriage, but he did not include any mention of God or any concept of an ultimate standard of morality. I sat there listening and praying that at least one student would get the message, but I wasn't all that hopeful. My fears were confirmed when the speaker ended his brief talk and opened the floor for questions. I sensed that what was about to happen would be awkward silence or something worse.

About halfway up the gym bleachers, an attractive older student stood and was called on to ask a question. She said, "I would never buy a car without insisting on a test-drive. Why wouldn't I do the same thing before I decided to spend my life with someone?" Before the speaker could answer, the students erupted with cheers. The question seemed to surprise him, because he struggled to answer, and the noise in the room drowned out most of his words. The uproar finally settled down, but there were no more questions. From the students' perspective, the case was closed.

When the assembly was dismissed, I approached several students I knew, and the young lady with the question happened to be standing there. She was still receiving compliments for her excellent question. I said to her, "Do you mind if I clear up one thing? In your question, are you always the test-driver or the car being test-driven? And does it make a difference? I mean, what happens if you test drive the car and the car doesn't want you?" She didn't say a thing. I knew that she was smart enough to realize her way of thinking worked only if you treated other people as objects. The test-driving analogy of relationships doesn't feel so great if you're the car that keeps getting test-driven off a cliff.

I mention this story to illustrate how confused, messed-up, and twisted our society has become when dealing with sex. My guess is that no matter what your background, you have been exposed to more sexual content of various kinds than your parents can even imagine. Sex is everywhere, and most of the glimpses of it are not meant to demonstrate respect, honor, and value. Our culture has become saturated with pornography. Most of the computer screens you pass each day are a click away from graphic images of immorality. A November/December 2008 *Group* magazine article quoted a survey of six colleges in which the vast majority of guys (86 percent) admitted they had viewed pornographic images in the previous year. And 20 percent reported that they looked at porn almost every day. No wonder we feel surrounded and saturated!

But we still have to live in this culture and deal with what it throws at us. The question we want to answer in this chapter is "How can we live wisely in an environment filled with sexual temptation?"

Before we look at this question through the perspective of the Choice Matrix, let's remind ourselves that God gives us permission to be hopeful about temptation:

> *No test or temptation that comes your way is beyond*
> *the course of what others have had to face. All you*
> *need to remember is that God will never let you*
> *down; he'll never let you be pushed past your limit;*
> *he'll always be there to help you come through it.*
> *(1 Corinthians 10:13)*

Also, although it may be natural to think of temptation as *sexual* temptation, it's wiser to think in the wider category of *sensual* temptation. Our senses and feelings are the primary channels through which temptation gains access to the decision-making part of us. Yes, there are *thought* temptations, such as doubts, intellectual questions, and fantasies, but if you consider them for a moment, most of them can be traced back to an emotional hook. How many people do you think struggle with doubts about Christianity because down deep they want to be accepted by people they know have rejected Christianity? To what degree do your questions about God have their root in disappointments with God or anger at him? How often do feelings of insecurity cause you to seek or hold on to objects or people who cannot really offer you security? Our senses, especially in our "Feelings rule" society, can be in charge of our lives, and it's not surprising that the results are a train wreck.

The Choice Matrix gives us a set of controls for living and for decision making that can operate above our feelings. These principles can overrule what we feel like doing.

#1: Trust God from the bottom of your heart.

Our senses are among God's gifts to us. Like all God's gifts, they have specific purposes and are not intended to be used outside of God's direction. Our senses can and should be trained. As a little child standing by the side of the road, you could see the cars coming by rapidly, but you didn't necessarily equate that perception with danger. The whole realization that "hard-things-coming-at-me-at-high-speed-will-hurt-if-I-don't-avoid-them" was not instinctive; it had to be trained. Hopefully, long before you stepped in front of a speeding car, you had the progressive experience of a door swinging in your direction or a wooden toy flung at you by another kid and you concluded that you didn't want to be on the receiving end of hard moving objects. Someone stood by the road with you and pointed out that the objects whizzing by weren't marshmallows or stuffed toys. You were told, "Listen, kid. If one of those hits you, it *will* hurt!"

Trusting God means letting him tell us about things that are beyond our senses. Trusting God means believing him when he tells us that something that doesn't *look* like a hard, painful experience headed toward us is actually something we should avoid. Trusting God from the bottom of our hearts means realizing that a package with pleasure written all over it in words and pictures may actually contain a lifetime of regrets, sickness, and even death. The human author of the Choice Matrix made a wise observation about sexual temptation:

> *The lips of a seductive woman are oh so sweet,*
> *her soft words are oh so smooth.*

> *But it won't be long before she's gravel in your mouth,*
> *a pain in your gut, a wound in your heart.*
> *(Proverbs 5:3-4)*

Solomon wasn't against sex; he was warning about the dangers of sex used as a way to control, manipulate, and destroy others.

The world doesn't like to wait. *We* don't like to wait. And when it comes to sex, the world tries hard to convince us that when God says, "Wait," he really means, "No." Because the world's spokespeople refuse to accept the idea that God invented sex, it's not surprising that they would reject the idea that God's plan for sex would be right, good, and the most fulfilling in the long run. They don't trust God, as a general rule, so they can't imagine trusting God with an area that has become the center of many people's lives.

So what does the world trust? They trust their feelings. Phrases like "Trust your heart" are spoken as if they convey an absolute truth and dependable guidance. But feelings are all about the moment. The most overwhelming and demanding feelings can be a faint memory from one minute to the next. Feelings are never the best reason to do anything. Yet the world not only tells us to trust our feelings but also informs us that we should never question those who encourage us to trust our feelings.

The ridiculous nature of the situation was pointed out by a friend of mine who drives a large old pickup truck with a heavy-duty bumper. He confessed to me that on more than one occasion, he has had a difficult choice when he finds himself driving behind someone with a bumper sticker that says, "If it feels good, do it!" When he reads those words, he suddenly has a strong desire to crumple the rear end of the other car with his truck. He thinks it would be great to pull over after the collision and meet the irate driver who would be demanding to know why my friend had been so rude. He'd say, "I read your bumper sticker and I thought it would feel good, so I did it!" Obviously, the proud owner of the bumper sticker really doesn't mean what he is proclaiming. What he means is, "If something feels good to me, I'm going to do it. But if something feels good to you, check with me before you do it."

It turns out that trusting our feelings over trusting God is the ultimate expression of self-centered living. Allowing our feelings, especially our hormone-driven feelings, to have the last word will get us in trouble too often to make that approach a wise one.

#2: Don't try to figure out everything on your own.

All of what you just read was preliminary to an unfortunate but likely truth: Right now in your life you are probably dealing with more guilt than questions when it comes to sex. At the close of your high school experience, you may already be carrying a weight of shame and doubt about what you have seen, thought about, or done. You may have read the opening paragraphs of this chapter with the thought, *Yeah, all this might be right, but it's too late for me.*

In the last couple of decades, the emphasis in official conversations with teens about sex has gradually shifted from information to intervention. As a friend of mine said, "I realize I don't often get an opportunity to warn inexperienced young people about wisdom, caution, and danger when it comes to sex. Kids aren't asking me many questions about sex; they're desperate to know what to do now that they're messed up because of it." The tragedy is that inside too many graduation caps and gowns walk young people who feel deeply damaged and perhaps beyond repair. All the talk about success at the end of high school sounds hollow if the person knows he or she is also carrying a lot of painful failures into the future. But, keep reading. Even if what I've described fits your feelings and experience, I've got some hopeful news for you.

Wisdom realizes that we can't figure our way out of sin. The second line in the Choice Matrix says, "Don't try to figure out everything on your own." But when we're struggling with guilt, it's tempting to sneak our way out of the problem. Coming up with excuses doesn't work and throwing in the towel doesn't work either. Isn't it amazing how something that looks so tempting and delightful one moment turns into a nightmare the next? Why is that? It isn't because sex itself is a bad thing; it's because something good is being offered in the wrong way or for the wrong reasons. Giving in to those temptations often seems nice at the time but quickly turns into something we regret. What we are experiencing is the two-step tactic that Satan uses: Step one is to temp; step two is to shame and enslave us if we yield. Satan first tried this tactic with our earliest ancestors and it worked so well that's he's been using it ever since. He got Adam and Eve to let their senses have the last word ("Boy, that fruit looks like it would be tasty! Is God keeping something good from us?")

and then immediately followed up with overwhelming feelings of guilt that caused them to be afraid of God.

Each time we do what we know is wrong or fail to live up to what we know is true, we can expect to "hear" Satan confirming our decision or trying to make us believe we have stepped over a line with God and there's no turning back. His purpose is clear: Once we're defeated, he wants to keep us that way for as long as possible. Then he wants to make us decide that the next best plan is to just keep on sinning. Satan's voice is not the voice we want to give our attention to.

The second part of the Choice Matrix reminds us that it isn't up to us to figure it out. We can express our trust in the Lord from the bottom of our hearts by listening to his instructions when we find ourselves in confusing and tempting situations. We learn to deal with temptation, and we learn that when we fail, we can still find acceptance and forgiveness with God. There's an amazing little passage the apostle Paul wrote down for young Timothy to help him remember how things work with God:

> *This is a sure thing:*
>> *If we die with him, we'll live with him;*
>> *If we stick it out with him, we'll rule with him;*
>> *If we turn our backs on him, he'll turn his back on*
>>> *us;*
>> *If we give up on him, he does not give up—*
>>> *for there's no way he can be false to himself.*
>>> *(2 Timothy 2:11-13)*

The first two "ifs" are positive promises, giving us good reasons to hang in there. The third "if" is a negative promise, warning us that if we insist on giving up, there's not much God can do about that. And the fourth "if" is an unexpected promise that during those moments when we are tempted to throw in the towel and give up, God still doesn't give up on us. We can't figure out why God would go that far, but he does. It's a God thing that we can always count on.

So before we move on to talking about some practical ways to deal with present and future temptations, let's pause to consider what we can do with the temptations with which we've already experienced failure. God hasn't given up on you, and you can't give up on yourself. If you are reading this, that means you're alive. And if you're alive, God can still do something very special with you, even if you've already failed miserably in your own eyes. In cases like your life and mine, God starts with forgiveness. First John 1:9 says, "If we admit our sins — make a clean breast of them — he won't let us down; he'll be true to himself. He'll forgive our sins and purge us of all wrongdoing." If you can honestly admit you feel defeated and hopeless, God's offer of forgiveness has to be good news. If there are specific failures that come to mind, reject any thought that those put you beyond God's ability to forgive. Offer those things to God in prayer and say to him, "Lord, these terrible things I have done are the very things for which I need forgiveness, and there's nothing I can do to deserve your mercy. I'm asking for it based on who you are, not who I am." Now think carefully. This brings us right back to the first point in the Choice Matrix.

Trusting God from the bottom of your heart means, in part, to trust him to forgive you. You must begin to think the incredible thought that even though you have messed up big-time, he will forgive you because you admitted your sin and asked for what he promised. Now you can get on with living!

#3: Listen for God's voice in everything you do, everywhere you go.

People struggling with temptation or the after-effects of failure report that it isn't easy to listen for God's voice: "How can I hear what God is saying in the middle of temptation when I can hardly hear *myself* think?"

Trying to listen to several voices is a real problem for many of us, and it's probably the reason God not only spoke to us but also had much of what he has to say written down. Does God still speak to us by his Holy Spirit? Certainly. But the "voice" we hear in any situation might not be the Holy Spirit. It may be our own mind playing tricks on us, or it may be Satan arranging a persuasive thought. So how do we tell if we're hearing God? We check what we're hearing with what God says in Scripture.

When does reading become listening? If we remember what we read, we can "hear" the words echoing in our heads. Part of the reason we are looking at various areas of life through the lens of a Matrix from God's Word is to build into our thinking a way to listen for God's voice in everything we do and everywhere we go.

God's Word is filled with direct instruction and personal examples regarding temptation. The Bible basically begins with original temptation (see Genesis 3) and ends with the banishment of temptation (see Revelation 22:15). In the lives of the people in Scripture, we find three major strategies to deal effectively with temptation: resistance, removal, and run!

Jesus got a full dose of temptation. Offers to sin came at him from every direction, but he resisted. The Bible tells us that there isn't a sin we face that when we talk to Jesus about it he can't say, "Been there, faced that." He understands from experience, not theory. "We don't have a priest who is out of touch with our reality. He's been through weakness and testing, experienced it all — all but the sin. So let's walk right up to him and get what he is so ready to give. Take the mercy, accept the help" (Hebrews 4:15-16).

How did Jesus practice resistance? He responded to temptation with Scripture. Matthew 4:1-11 describes Jesus' encounter with Satan in the wilderness. The environment was a sensual battlefield. Jesus was hungry, lonely, and tired. Three times Satan took a run at him, and each time he answered the "offer" by relying on what God said. Even when Satan mockingly tried to twist what God said (the tactic he also did with Eve), Jesus came back with the truth.

Resistance must be one of our tactics. James tells us, "Let God work his will in you. Yell a loud *no* to the Devil and watch him scamper" (4:7). This tactic works, but most of us have to learn to use it more consistently. In the meantime, we need to remember the other two options: removal and run.

King David failed to practice removal, and the consequences created a disaster in his life and his family. Removal has to do with taking out sources of temptation from our lives or not going where we know we will be tempted. If we have the option to go or not go somewhere where we know we will be tempted and we go anyway, we are subtly choosing to fail before we've even been tempted.

King David was bored one night in his entertainment room (the palace roof), so he began to channel surf. He clicked the remote as he walked around the edges of the roof until he found "adult entertainment," a beautiful woman taking a bath in one of the adjoining homes. David saw her and then kept looking. After a while, he decided to find out who she was. Then he arranged for them to meet. That highly charged encounter led to an explosive moral failure that literally blew up David's family (see 2 Samuel 11–12).

David was in the wrong place at the wrong time and failed to practice removal. He was careless about temptation and it trapped him. When we keep things around that we know represent temptation to us, we will make it harder on ourselves to practice resistance. Anytime we are on the Internet, we are almost in the same situation David put himself. If we're not careful where we're going, we'll end up on sites that are as tempting and destructive as the view from David's deck.

Joseph had a different problem. He was minding his own business and someone came after him. He couldn't remove himself and he practiced resistance, but the wife of his employer had her own agenda and was persistent. Things reached critical mass when Potiphar's wife laid a trap for Joseph and tried to lure him into her bed. At that point, Joseph had no choice but tactic number three: He ran! (see Genesis 39:12). Now, it's worth remembering that running got Joseph *out* of temptation, but it got him *into* trouble. The "rejected" woman tried to destroy him. If you run from temptation, you might have to face ridicule and misunderstanding. But Joseph is an example of the ups and downs of trusting God from the bottom of our hearts. It won't always be easy, but if we persist, things will turn out in the end. Joseph kept listening to God more closely than he "listened" to his circumstances, and God fulfilled his promises.

#4: He's the one who will keep you on track.

Most of us have to learn by experience to be more like Joseph. We usually get the arrangement turned completely around. We think that if God will make everything turn out all right for me, then I'll trust him. What we're saying is, "God, make my life such that I never have to really trust you and then I'll trust you." In the Choice Matrix, we're reminded that Trust comes first and Track comes last. If we're not trusting, we can't honestly expect God to keep us on track.

If that last paragraph sounds as though God isn't being fair, think again. Trust comes first because that's how we enter the picture. But the truth is that long before we get around to trusting, God has already demonstrated his trustworthiness over and over. The very fact that we get the opportunity to trust is evidence of God's faithfulness. If he didn't want to give us the chance, we'd never get around to trusting him.

Most of us can grasp the concept that the person most worth trusting is the person who loves us the most. Because they love us, they have our best interests at heart. If we know they love us, we can continue to trust them even when we don't understand immediately why they might choose to say or do certain things. God has demonstrated he is the one who loves us most and can be trusted from the bottom of our hearts. "God put his love on the line for us by offering his Son in sacrificial death while we were of no use whatever to him" (Romans 5:8). Survival in the sex-saturated wilderness will always come back to trusting God with everything we've got.

WISE BITES

"Be careful! Relationships are portrayed as easy, casual things, but good ones take maturity and effort. Never settle."

"I wish I had been told that waiting to date would save me a lot of trouble."

"I was not ready for a dating relationship when I left home. I know we all mature at different rates, but believe me, a couple years down the road you will look back and see how much you've grown and wonder why on earth you thought you were emotionally, spiritually, and mentally prepared for something as big as a serious relationship."

FRIENDS, ROOMMATES, AND OTHER CLOSE ENCOUNTERS

You who are young, make the most of your youth.
Relish your youthful vigor.
Follow the impulses of your heart.
If something looks good to you, pursue it.
But know also that not just anything goes;
You have to answer to God for every last bit of it.

ECCLESIASTES 11:9

I asked a number of college students from the University of Wisconsin-Oshkosh to answer the question, "Now that you have been away from home for a while, what do you wish someone had talked to you about before you left for college?"

One student wrote this about her experience with friends and roommates:

Relating to friends and roommates was what I was least prepared for when I left home. Seeking the approval from my peers was my biggest weakness when I first entered college. I remember the summer before my freshman year my being so stressed out about my roommate situation and meeting new friends that I kind of developed an apathy toward God's will. I took my social life into my own hands and didn't acknowledge that God was in control. I believe that Satan had a huge part in this weakness of my life, and he is fully capable of filling high school graduates with a fear of rejection that can blind them from God's control. Satan definitely blinded me from the blessings God could have given me my first year, and I wish I would have known how important it was to place my social life in God's hands. I am currently in my sophomore year, and by God's grace and patience, he has given me another chance to give it over to him. Ever since I handed this area of my life over to God, he has blessed me with abundance beyond what I could ask for, including Bible studies and fellowship. I may have missed out on a year of this, but God has taught me how important it is to give him control of every area of my life. He gives us so much peace when we just trust that he will take

care of our every need. But to fully experience this,
we need to let go and let God.

This student learned some valuable lessons the hard way. As you read her note, you might have noticed aspects of the Choice Matrix coming through. Trusting God from the bottom of our hearts is certainly a place where many people come back to and say, "Here's where I turned off on a detour." Realize that you will probably also learn at least some unexpected lessons as you work on your life. Some of them will be hard—and unforgettable. You will find you're not ready for everything, but that's part of the adventure. One reason you're reading this book is probably because you realize it might not be all that great to simply repeat everyone else's mistakes. If you're going to make mistakes along the way, make them your own.

When it comes to mistakes, a good strategy has three parts: first, avoid obvious mistakes; second, really learn from the mistakes you do make; and third, share your wisdom from your mistakes with someone else. You will observe that people around you will often brag about their mistakes and never get around to saying what they actually learned or how they benefited from trying to go without sleep for three days in a row or something far more risky.

#1: Trust God from the bottom of your heart.

Going off to school or the military or simply moving away from home usually comes with its own set of anxieties and concerns. You will be exposed to more strangers than you've ever had to deal with before. High school may have placed you in classes with lots of different people, but you didn't have to live with them. At the end of a stressful day, you could still go back to the familiar environment called home. Suddenly, that will not be nearly as much an option if you go away to school.

Most colleges and universities try to offer a system that lets you determine the kind of roommate you will end up with in the dorm. The systems aren't perfect. It isn't unusual for roommates to agree after a year that the match didn't work. When you are filling out rooming preference forms, be as specific as possible and make your answers about yourself honest.

The situation is more complicated if you are living on your own and have to find one or more roommates to make a rental house or multiple-bedroom apartment affordable. There are websites now that assist with the search and do some of the screening, but sharing a roof with a stranger usually involves a certain amount of culture clash. Your lifestyle, as normal and comfortable as it may seem to you, will probably seem foreign to someone else, even if you've both been raised in the same country or state. You will simply discover that the way you've grown up isn't the way everyone else grew up, and when it comes to laundry, cleanliness, cooking and eating habits, and so on, you and your roommates might feel as though you've been raised on separate planets. Some of these differences can be worked out, but sometimes they cause a separation. All these occurrences can turn into healthy lessons for later in life. One current college student wrote a succinct philosophy for dealing with roommates: "Be friendly. Chill out. The most problems I see in friendships/roommate relationships are the consequence of uptightness in the relationship. If everyone just cooled off, didn't freak out about things that were not freak-out worthy, there wouldn't be roommate troubles."

Leaving home does get you into some unusual circumstances. The following young man's experience may give you some good pointers about friends, roommates, and other close encounters as you embark on life on your own.

Dan got a great scholarship to a prestigious university. It was one of those dream all-expenses-paid deals. Under normal circumstances, he probably wouldn't have accepted the offer because his family was well-off and he could have chosen to go to any school. But shortly before Dan left home, his family went through a difficult time and was wiped out financially. Suddenly the scholarship was an offer Dan couldn't refuse, and off he went. As things turned out, Dan never returned home again, although he thought often about his old neighborhood and the special lessons he had learned about God in those streets and alleyways.

Dan's new school put all the scholarship students in the same fraternity. They were offered a pampered life. Most of the incoming freshmen were from wealthy and connected families, but this frat house was more like a palace. The school had hired staff for the house that waited hand and foot on the students. One of Dan's happy discoveries when he arrived at B.U. was that three of his friends from home were also given scholarships, so he wasn't alone right from the start. But there was a not-so-happy discovery when Dan realized that the fraternity had a food policy that was very different from the diet he was familiar with at home. It wasn't bad food, just very different. This was a mini-crisis. The temptation to blend in and live it up was strong. The tantalizing smells from the kitchen and the sounds of raucous drinking from the well-stocked frat bar seemed like an irresistible invitation to live it up. Dan didn't want to create problems for the cook at the fraternity, but he wanted to stay true to his convictions, too. The question for Dan boiled down to "Does it matter what I eat or drink?"

Actually, when you leave home, the first three words in Dan's question will become the start of a fill-in-the-blank question that you will use almost every day: Does it matter _____? As in, "Does it matter who I spend my time with? Does it matter how I keep my room? Does it matter what study habits I develop? Does it matter how I act when no one who knows me is watching?" For most people, answering those questions means assuming that each one actually means, "Does it matter *to me* who, what, or if?" That's not how Dan saw the question. His question was, "Does it matter *to God* what I do and the way I live?"

For Dan, trusting God meant that the choices he made about every part of life needed to be in harmony with God's desires. Dan understood a principle Jesus illustrated in one of his parables when he talked about God's response to those who take care of small important matters: "Good servant! Great work! Because you've been trustworthy in this small job, I'm making you governor of ten towns" (Luke 19:17). The real issue wasn't about food but about Dan living a life that honored God first. So he had to propose a plan that would allow him to avoid compromising himself while at the same time maintaining his relationship with those around him.

The frat cook liked Dan, but he was afraid that if Dan and his friends ate a different diet, their health would suffer and he would then get into big trouble. So Dan implemented the second phase of the Choice Matrix.

#2: Don't try to figure out everything on your own.

We sometimes think it would be easier to trust God if we just knew how he's going to intervene or what his plan of action will be. But God consistently shows us that trusting him usually involves *not knowing* what he is going to do, but trusting him anyway. Dan's strategy created room for God to work. He told the cook, "Look, if you'll let my friends and I design our own menu for ten days and anyone thinks we're losing ground in our health, we'll eat what everyone else is eating."

So while everyone else was OD-ing on burgers, fries, pizza, and beer, Dan and his friends ate a fresh diet of vegetables. Ten days later, when their frat-mates were looking a little fat and lazy, Dan and his friends were the picture of health. After that, the cook let them determine their own diet. This was the beginning of an amazing career for Dan in public service, and his life on his own was rooted in those first choices he made when he left home. By the way, if you want to read Dan's whole story, check out the book of Daniel in the Old Testament.

The point of leaving home to live on your own or to go to school is not to simply exchange one life for another. There are values, lessons, truth, relationships, and wisdom that are absolutely worth keeping in the move. It's exciting to be on your own; it's a lot like crawling out onto the limb of a tree that is waving in the breeze. Most of us experience a thrill in a new environment with a different perspective on our past. The experience is exhilarating. But the idea that the next move is to saw off the branch you're resting on because the rest of the tree is the past and no longer important really doesn't make all that much sense.

#3: Listen for God's voice in everything you do, everywhere you go.

Without even trying, roommates, new friends, and acquaintances in your life will challenge your way of thinking. They will make you question your assumptions. They will make you doubt and perhaps even cause you to change some of your beliefs about life and people. But here's a startling thought: God is allowing each of these people into your life. This doesn't mean they are necessarily offering you something good or true, but it does mean that good can come from your interaction with them. As one current college student put it, "Don't be afraid to interact with your roommate. Your roommate may become your best friend or your worst enemy, an honest ally or a well-meaning flatterer, but you won't know the nature of that relationship until you actually build one."

One lesson God allows us to learn repeatedly throughout life is that we are not the center of the universe. In a certain way, roommates are God's messengers to drive home that point. As another college student put it, "Roommates can have a lot to teach you about learning to get along with different kinds of people. Make sure to be open to what they can teach you." This might seem obvious, but our current culture's view of relationships is almost directly opposite to God's perspective on them. The world tells us to come up with a list of all the qualities we're looking for in a roommate and keep changing them until we find one that meets all the qualities on that list. We even apply this approach to looking for a mate. But Jesus says, "Here is a simple, rule-of-thumb guide for behavior: Ask yourself what you want people to do for you, then grab the initiative and do it for *them*. Add up God's Law and Prophets and this is what you get" (Matthew 7:12). The crucial question isn't "What kind of roommate do I want?" but "What kind of roommate am I willing to be?" The experience of many others will tell you that you will probably not find an ideal roommate. You have limited control over those circumstances. But you do have a lot of control over the kind of roommate you will be. You will find that it doesn't take much effort to think about the things your roommate does that get on your nerves. It will take real effort to be honest about what you do that gets on your roommate's nerves — and to be willing to do something about those actions. But this is the area that God is very interested in talking to you about. He's not nearly as interested in hearing you pray about all the ways you want to revise and rebuild your roommate as he is about hearing you thank him for the good (though sometimes painful) lessons he is allowing you to learn through that person.

#4: He's the one who will keep you on track.

College roommates aren't permanent, but the lessons we learn through them can be. Life after school will put you in constant situations where you'll have to be able to get along with people who are not like you. It comes as a shock to people that what they remember most about college isn't necessarily the knowledge learned or the academic skills developed. What they remember are the people and the relationships that grew during those years. One student wrote,

> *Your friends are the best part of college. I highly recommend staying loyal to these people, and even if they're doing things you don't approve of, have a frank talk with them instead of talking behind their backs. The same goes for the inevitable conflict that occurs when you spend a great deal of your time with the same people. If you have a problem with someone, just let the person know instead of bottling it up and eventually ending your friendship because of irreconcilable differences. The secret I've learned in my relationships is to pretend that everyone is going to die in the next half hour. Then I'm a lot less likely to say nasty things to them!*

No matter what your various experiences with roommates are, try to remember that God is using these fun and hard moments to keep you on track. He has a purpose in mind for you and it involves developing in you the character of Jesus. Friends and roommates represent God's relationship lab in your life. Not every experiment or theory will work out the way you expected, but even failures have a way of teaching us and keeping us on track.

One way to recognize the pattern God is working out in your life already is to think about the ways your relationships in high school have shaped you. Identify some of the people issues that have taught you about what it means to be like Jesus and perhaps some of the areas where you have a long way to go. Your friendships in high school may have forced you to discover a streak of impatience or quick anger in yourself. Those same relationships may have also revealed that you have a knack for compassion—for encouraging people in tough situations. You can already recognize in yourself certain traits that will require self-control, while others need to be practiced more often with those around you.

As you move out on your own and relate to people, these same characteristics will continue to be refined and God will continue to use people to keep you on track. The kind of development work God is doing in your life will go a lot smoother if you keep the opening phrase of the Choice Matrix as the screen saver in your mind: Trust in the Lord from the bottom of your heart.

 BITES

"Your first roommate usually won't be your best friend."

"There will be bad roommates. Regardless of who it is, you have to be able to communicate your needs so that you can have a happy and healthy college career."

"Even if they are your best friends ever, it still might not be the best idea to room with them. Some people make better friends than roommates; some people make better roommates than friends."

FAMILY STILL COUNTS

He will convince parents to look after their children and children to look up to their parents. If they refuse, I'll come and put the land under a curse.

MALACHI 4:6

When I think of family, I think about my own, of course, but I also think of Joe's. His home was a perfect example of the old saying "You can pick your friends, but you can't pick your family; friends come and go, but family is for keeps." This saying reveals something about how we feel about our families, but sometimes it also reminds us about how our family feels about us. After all, they didn't get to pick us, either.

Born as almost the youngest in a large family, Joe had to struggle to be noticed by his older brothers. But for some strange reason, Joe and his father had a special relationship. Perhaps an explanation for their unique bond is that Joe's was a blended family, and Joe was the firstborn of his father's second wife.

In this case, the blending was about as extreme as it gets, with children from four different women being raised under the same roof. And the older kids resented the fact that their father had a definite favorite among his children. Joe got gifts from his dad that were not given to the rest of the family. For his own part, Joe didn't seem aware of his special position and didn't really understand the depth of his siblings' envy. So he made things worse by telling his brothers things they really didn't want to hear. He had dreams about his future in which he was basically the leader of the family, and when he described these dreams to his brothers, their resentment got worse. Joe didn't notice the hate-filled glint in their eyes or the nods and looks his brothers exchanged. He didn't see the trouble coming. We'll see what happened a little later.

Your family is unique more than it's strange. We tend to see most other families as being somewhat alike, but the flaws and idiosyncrasies of our family stick out like sore thumbs. We might take the good parts of our family life for granted and assume that we haven't had anything special because "all families are that way." The "different" or messed-up parts of our family can easily become an embarrassment to us. In any case, it is difficult to really see our own family dynamics. After all, looking at family is somewhat self-examination. We're part of what we are trying to see. We can separate ourselves only so far, and the tools we use to look at our families will help or hinder us from seeing the truth. Seeing your family clearly is a lot like trying to look at your own face without using a mirror. But distance sometimes gives us a new perspective. One of the shocking discoveries we make when we are out on our own is that our family might have been amazing in some unexpected ways.

When I was in college, I often visited home on the weekends because I not only enjoyed my mother's cooking but also looked forward to the long conversations we had around the table after meals. As my younger brothers and sister grew up, this became a habit. Sometimes the meals led into an hour or two of interaction before the dishes got picked up and cleaned. I now realize that my parents have a unique gift of hospitality.

I realized the power of these times on one occasion when one of my brothers brought home a kid for supper who had just been released from prison. The teenager had obviously had a rough life, and my brother's own flirting with rebellion had created camaraderie between them. My brother had his own agenda for the evening and hadn't planned to stick around long after supper, but the conversation around the table took off and the stranger among us was mesmerized. I don't remember what we were talking about, but the kid had obviously never sat in on stimulating family interaction before. He was like a moth flitting around a candle, drawn to the light.

My brother kept hinting that it was time for them to go, but this kid didn't want to break the spell. He had been welcomed into a circle at that table where love was real and interest in one another was genuine. The experience touched a deep need in him. For my brother, this was the usual. He could take it or leave it. It was easy for him (and me) to assume that the same atmosphere would be there tomorrow evening and the day after that. For the newcomer, family fellowship was a taste of living he had never had before. At one point, my brother tugged on his sleeve in an effort to move him away from the table. The boy looked at him and said, "You go ahead. I think I'm staying here."

I briefly interrupted Joe's story because one of the potential upsides of leaving home is a deepened appreciation for the gift of family. Whether leaving home is hard or easy for us, the distance can help us see things we didn't see close-up. We should make a special effort to notice the good things God brought into our lives through our families. But God has also wired us to leave at some point. We begin in the womb, graduate to the nest-like environment of home, and eventually are pushed over the edge or find our way out and take flight. Part of the transition from childhood to adulthood is leaving home in some way. When the Bible speaks about the basics of marriage, one of the essential components is a separation from Mom and Dad to form a new family: "Therefore a man leaves his father and mother and embraces his wife. They become one flesh" (Genesis 2:24). Even in cases like family farms and businesses, the transition between one generation and another doesn't happen automatically. There has to be intergenerational cooperation. Parents have to let go, and children have to leave. Those changes allow the relationships within a family to grow and mature.

A student from Houghton College wrote some wise counsel to people going away to school:

College is easier for you because you've left your old world and discovered a new one. Your family faces everyday life with a huge hole where you used to be. Respect that, and try to include them. Don't expect to be treated as an adult now that you've left home, because unless you're paying for college by yourself, you haven't yet earned the adult title. They still have the right to provide input and advice and even to straight-up tell you what you're going to do.

Clearly, leaving home is a process, not so much an event. Your physical absence may not mean that all the strings have been severed. You might (and should) continue to feel different kinds of connection with your family, although your new experiences and distance will inevitably alter the ways you and your family relate.

Because your relationship with your family has been one of the primary shaping influences in your life, it's important to apply the Choice Matrix in thinking through your ongoing interaction with your parents and siblings. And that also brings us back to Joe and his brothers.

#1: Trust God from the bottom of your heart.

When we left Joe's story, he was blithely going through life without suspecting that disaster was about to strike. His father unknowingly put his favorite son in harm's way. Joe's brothers were away on an extended business trip and Joe's father, Jake, sent him to check on how the older boys were doing. Far from home, the rules changed.

When Joe tracked down his brothers, they saw him coming and all the pent-up anger came to the surface. They had allowed things to get to the point where they wanted to kill their younger brother. Now, I realize that in our sibling squabbles we will often threaten all kinds of bodily harm to our brothers and sisters, but we usually don't mean it and we would be the first to leap to their defense if someone else tried to hurt them. But Joe's brothers meant business. The streak of mean in each of them came together into a raging river of hatred. Only one of them, the oldest, thought of a way they could get rid of Joe permanently and avoid having blood on their hands. They threw him into a dry well and were going to leave him to die (actually, the oldest brother was planning to spring Joe from the well later once he had learned his lesson). Then another brother spotted some traveling traders who dealt in human lives and came up with a "better" idea. Joe's brothers actually sold their little brother into slavery. Talk about leaving home! Departure by betrayal is about as bad as it gets.

We sense that up to this point in Joe's life, Dad was a big figure and God was a minor one. But once he was cut off from home, Joe focused on what he had left: his relationship with God. He began to apply the first phase of the Choice Matrix, trusting God from the bottom of his heart. Overnight he went from favorite in the family to slave. His life wasn't his, and his future looked hopeless. All he could rely on were God and a couple of amazing dreams related to his family. It was enough. The Bible tells us, "As it turned out, GOD was with Joseph and things went very well with him. He ended up living in the home of his Egyptian master" (Genesis 39:2). Joe's story takes place in the last twelve chapters of the book of Genesis.

One way to look at the rest of Joe's life is to see it as his patient effort to settle things with his brothers. Had they known he was alive (eventually, of course, they found out he was), they would have been worried that he might want to get even, and then some. But Joseph had something much more satisfying and freeing in mind for his brothers than getting even. He completely shocked them by forgiving them. And he was able to do that because of the relationship with God he developed through years as a slave, then as a prisoner, then as the second-in-charge of Egypt. He watched God bring his dreams to reality, and he realized they worked out in part because of his brothers' betrayal. God took something terrible in Joe's past and worked wonders with it because Joe kept on trusting from the bottom of his heart. Eventually he told his brothers, "Don't be afraid. Do I act for God? Don't you see, you planned evil against me but God used those same plans for my good, as you see all around you right now—life for many people" (Genesis 50:19-20).

Leaving home can be exciting, but it also has a traumatic side. Your departure will probably not be like Joe's, but there might be some intense feelings involved. The one who leaves is often surprised by feelings of loneliness. The overwhelming weight of new responsibilities may create the occasional wish to be a kid with no worries again. You might suspect that people back home aren't missing you nearly as much as they say. If Mom and Dad turn your bedroom into a fitness-and-entertainment center the week after you leave, it's not hard to figure out that the sense of newfound freedom you've been feeling cuts both ways.

Even if your room is kept as a shrine, going home is never quite the same. One student noted,

*The first time you go home after being away for a
while will tell you a lot about how things will go in
the future. When I first came home from college for
a quick weekend visit, the structure I had grown to
accept at school dissolved completely into the chaotic
"normality" of home. In the few short weeks I was
gone, everything had changed just enough to make me
uncomfortable. I didn't receive the reaffirmation that
I was seeking and ended up fighting with my parents
most of the weekend.*

*No matter how things go the first time you return
home, communication before, during, and after is key.
Without discussion and communication, my family
and I would not have been able to eventually work
out the negative emotions and misplaced expectations
that caused the heartache of my first visit home.*

Another way in which your departure will create a parallel experience with Joe's will involve the way your relationship with

God will come into focus as something separate from family faith. We will discuss this in greater length in the chapters on faith and church, but for now, realize that the ways you express your trust in God as an individual will have a profound effect on your family. If they are believers, they are hoping to see evidence that you are living out a relationship with God on your own. The best way to demonstrate this is by how you implement the second phase of the Choice Matrix in your conversations with the folks back home.

#2: Don't try to figure out everything on your own.

The best way to get people to treat you like an adult is to act like an adult. This may catch your parents by surprise. It will take time for them to grasp that you are more than their child. There are things they have always had to do for you that they will no longer have to do, and that takes some getting used to.

After my oldest son left for the military, a few weeks went by before he was able to call home. I knew he had been through some of the most intense and overwhelming experiences in his life in the days since he had left us. I was eager to hear him talk about all that he had learned. But I wasn't prepared for a question he asked early in the conversation: "So, Dad, how are you, really?" He was still calling me Dad, but he was talking to me as one adult talks to another. I couldn't remember him ever asking me how I was before. Kids usually don't ask their parents, "How are you doing?" But that simple question is one of the marks of adulthood: expressing genuine care and interest in someone else.

#3: Listen for God's voice in everything you do, everywhere you go.

One way we check how we're doing with trusting God from the bottom of our hearts is to do a spiritual hearing test once in a while. Ask yourself, *If I'm trusting God, when was the last time I did something because I was listening to him?* What we're doing with the wisdom we brought with us from home says a lot about how we are listening to God. As one student admitted,

> *For the first two years of college, I pretty much decided to ignore all the advice my family had given me and took a walk on the wild side instead. Fortunately, my family loved me anyway, and I am closer with them now than ever. Their love and God's patient work through circumstances (some of them painful) and in my heart brought me around.*

God never stops speaking to us as long as we are breathing. During those two years this young lady walked on the wild side, God never lost sight of her or ceased to speak into her life. His Word was nearby the whole time. There were probably some days when she had to work hard to ignore God. Taking a moment each day to acknowledge God is an important practice you can carry out to do your part in staying on track.

#4: He's the one who will keep you on track.

God didn't single out parents for one of the Ten Commandments, but he did single out every one of us as children. The fifth commandment takes on an added dimension when we move out of our childhood home: "Honor your father and mother so that you'll live a long time in the land that God, your God, is giving you" (Exodus 20:12). We never outgrow this commandment. Even when we are parents ourselves, we usually still have parents and grandparents with whom we are called to practice this commandment. It has often been observed that children learn best how to honor their parents as they observe the way their folks honor *their* parents.

One college student thoughtfully summarized the way honoring our parents can be an ongoing learning experience:

You can have the best relationship with your parents and going home will still be challenging. When you come back after having lived elsewhere, you have built for yourself a new support group and discovered a new world. It will be jarring going back to the old one. Also, you've met so many new people and gained new perspectives on life through them. You've also put some emotional distance between yourself and home, so when you go home, you will suddenly see little attitudes or behaviors or actions that your family members have that you no longer think are right or healthy. Don't let this opening of your eyes to the negative things at home drive you away from your family.

After I left home, I found myself making negative comments about my mom. I had to carefully examine why I was making these comments and I realized that

I was seeing things in my mother that really bothered me about me. I also thought about all the ways my mom is wonderful, and that helped balance out my negative observations.

You might find that loving your family becomes a bit of a chore for a while. It's hard, but I honestly believe that when love requires effort, it becomes something stronger and more real. So brave it out. Accept the challenge to allow your relationship with the members of your family to grow and mature so that even distance doesn't diminish what they mean to you.

As you move further into adulthood, your willingness to express respect and appreciation for your parents will have a profound impact on them. The commandment to respect them (see Exodus 20:12) has a promise connected to it, similar to the last phrase of the Choice Matrix. In the Choice Matrix, God promises to keep you on track; in the commandment, God promises long life in the land he gives. These phrases are different aspects of the same experience—God's blessing. Living under God's direction will result in good things in your life. God gives you permission to expect them.

Your high school graduation will be a lot about you. Don't forget where you came from and who helped you get there. Taking a moment to thank Mom and Dad specifically for ways they've helped you won't take away from your achievement; it will show that you are growing up the right way.

BITES

"Don't haul half the dorm home with you over Christmas break!"

"I wish my parents had understood that I was going to change and they were not going to understand the changes."

"Be aware that your family might be a little threatened when you come home with all this new knowledge. It doesn't matter how you view your behavior — if your family says you're treating them as if they're stupid, you need to tone down the academese."

PRACTICING INTEGRITY

His wife said, "Still holding on to your precious integrity, are you?
Curse God and be done with it!"

JOB 2:9

"**D**o you know your credit score?" As you move through
college and into your career, you will probably notice that
for many adults, the credit score has the same kind of effect that
your grade point average had while you were in high school. If
you have been making plans to go to college, you probably know
exactly what your GPA is right now. You may have sweated
out admission because you realized that your GPA was close
to the cutoff point your chosen school uses to decide whether
they will accept a lot of money from you for your ongoing

education. Meanwhile, if your parents are planning to help you with college, they might be sweating out their credit scores.

We'll discuss this in more length in the chapter pertaining to money, but for now it's worth noting that at least three huge companies in our country make it their business to give almost every person a fluctuating grade or score for how they use credit. The scale these companies use is based, like baseball batting averages, on one thousand. In credit score language, a great batting average such as .400 doesn't mean much. Credit scores start looking impressive when they are over .700. The questions worth asking about credit scores are the same ones we instinctively ask about grade point averages: How important is this, really, and why?

Even if you have a perfect 4.0 (or 5.0) GPA, it's likely that the idea of being reduced or measured by a number is a little frustrating to you. If it has been a struggle for you to maintain your GPA at average or above, the narrow value on your life might have you wanting to bang your head against the wall sometimes. You may find it hard not to resent people who seem to coast along to good grades while you agonize to get passing grades. You would be all for every GPA having a footnote stating, "The number recorded above does not represent everything about this person."

Grade point averages and credit scores have several things in common. They both seem to offer an effective way to measure for the purposes of comparison. There's more about you that you wish could be taken into account, but grades and credit record seem to be among those things that can actually be counted.

They represent a kind of measurable treasure — something you've earned. You may want to say that there's more about you to consider, but someone who's into GPAs will probably ask, "Well, how do you measure the rest of you?" They might even try to put you on the spot and ask, "What *is* more important than GPAs and credit scores, and can that be measured?" The one-word answer to the first part of that question is *integrity*, and the answer to the second part of the question is that integrity can certainly be recognized even if it can't be precisely measured.

Integrity has to do with what we say and how we act. Do our words and actions harmonize? Can people count on what we promise to do? Note that GPAs and credit scores do attempt to measure a thin slice of integrity. GPAs measure how well we do at the duty of study. The grades we get are supposed to reflect our efforts to carry out our promise to study. Likewise, credit scores are supposed to reflect how well we do at paying what we promise to pay. If our performance doesn't match our promises, our score goes down.

People recognize your level of integrity when they think about how closely your actions match your promises. Are you a person whose word can be trusted? The older you get, the more significant the issue of personal integrity will become. Up until now, people have probably cut you a lot of slack because you are young and still learning what you can and can't promise. Later there will be a lot less slack to cut. People will expect you to follow through. If you don't, consequences will follow. If you get hired for a job that requires you to show up at 8 a.m. and you make it a habit of arriving at 8:15 or 8:30, you won't have the job very long.

The fact is that right now, people seem to care a lot more about GPAs and credit scores than about personal integrity. This boils down to a widely held belief that feelings trump promises. In other words, no matter what I promise to do, I don't actually have to do it if I don't feel like it. People who try this with their credit scores get in trouble fast: "Yes, I know I promised to pay my rent on the first day of every month, but I didn't feel like it this month. I went shopping with my rent money instead, and then I felt a lot better." To which the response will be something like, "How do you feel without a roof over your head?"

Ultimately, integrity builds up to some major promises in life that need to be kept. This takes us back to some words Jesus said about the connection between integrity in small issues and integrity on the major promises in life. He said, "Good servant! Great work! Because you've been trustworthy in this small job, I'm making you governor of ten towns" (Luke 19:17). Every small promise and commitment you make (and keep) is developing a track record of integrity in your life. People notice; they remember.

You can probably see how this principle works in your relationship with your parents in the area of trust. Trust is hard to earn, easy to destroy. And nothing demolishes trust like not keeping your promises. We get into trouble with our parents when we make promises but then treat every situation like an exception: "Yes, I know I promised to have the car back at eleven, but I forgot to wear my watch and lost track of time. I couldn't help it." Or "I know I promised for the fifth day in a row to mow the grass, but for the fifth day in a row, something came up." Integrity is a pattern of promises kept, not a pile of broken promises based on exceptions. Your parents would have a definite answer to the question if you asked them, "Do I tend to keep or break my promises?" That answer would give you an accurate reading of your level of integrity. If you know that your parents would have to respond with low marks for your integrity track record, this is an area that needs special attention in your life.

#1: Trust God from the bottom of your heart.

Developing integrity isn't the quest for perfection; it involves recognizing mistakes and knowing what to do about them. One of the best examples of youthful integrity can be found in the parable Jesus told about the two brothers who were asked by their dad to help him work in the fields. He got two different responses:

> "He went up to the first and said, 'Son, go out for the
> day and work in the vineyard.'
>> "The son answered, 'I don't want to.' Later on he
>> thought better of it and went.
> "The father gave the same command to the second
>> son. He answered, 'Sure, glad to.' But he
>> never went.
> "Which of the two sons did what the father asked?"
> They said, "The first." (Matthew 21:28-31)

Jesus used this parable to point out that many people reject God's approach at first but later realize that they really do need him. He was confronting people who easily say yes to God but then don't follow up with their lives at all. He went on to tell his audience,

Yes, and I tell you that crooks and whores are going to precede you into God's kingdom. John came to you showing you the right road. You turned up your noses at him, but the crooks and whores believed him. Even when you saw their changed lives, you didn't care enough to change and believe him. (Matthew 21:31-32)

Trusting God from the bottom of your heart is a matter of integrity. It's not about *feeling* trusting but about *living* trusting. We've touched on this in many ways already, but leaving home will clarify your actual level of trust in God. You will have the chance to discover how much of your trust in God was simply a part of your home and family environment and how much of that trust is your own, apart from your surroundings.

Life at home means, in part, not having to trust God all that much. Your direct needs are met by your parents, so it's a little harder to think that your parents are actually part of God showing himself faithful in your life. You might be surrounded by friends at school and church and therefore haven't had to take much of an active part in pursuing relationships or trusting God in new situations. But when you are on your own, immediate dependence on God becomes more of an issue. Days become filled with opportunities to rely on him for work, wisdom in school, handling new challenges, and making significant decisions. Integrity has to do with being clear that you *are* going to rely on God. Pretending to trust God isn't going to take you very far.

Trusting in God also works its way into how we practice integrity with other people. Integrity in human relationships means we aren't trying to manage or manipulate other people. It means we know we're not responsible for their responses and behavior, so we keep entrusting them to God and work at being honest with them. It means we're not just pretending to be someone we think they will like, but we are running the risk of being ourselves even if they decide not to like us. Practicing integrity means that we'll entrust God with a lot of life and not try to figure everything out on our own.

#2: Don't try to figure out everything on your own.

Telling the truth to people doesn't mean we tell everyone everything about everything. It does mean that what we decide to tell people is the truth. That way, we don't have to keep a lot of stories straight. As one student summarized it, "Be as honest as possible without sharing stuff that is none of people's business." Another cautioned about sharing truthfully but with reasonable caution: "Realize that not everyone is trustworthy and that it is easy to get a reputation in an environment like college. Also, remember that the person who is your best friend right now may not be so close to you later, so watch how much you reveal."

For many people, moving onto a college or university campus is a chance to start over in life. They might be tempted to reinvent themselves. After all, there may not be anyone else at this school that knew them back home. Responses from a number of college students were almost unanimous in saying, "Keep away from being dishonest about your past. Better to keep quiet than to tell what isn't true. Those lies always come back to haunt you in some way."

Integrity involves learning to be comfortable with the core of who you are and working on the changes that can and need to be made. It doesn't mean that your past doesn't include sadness or wounds that you don't think will ever heal, but it does mean that you turn over to God those parts of yourself that you can't figure out and leave them in his hands.

Getting through college doesn't mean you've reached the end of learning. In fact, most of what you think you really know in college will get edited in the real world when you get out. But those years will refine your learning style and will walk you through the first steps of life on your own. People who float through college as a series of classes and assignments without thinking about the direction of their lives have wasted a lot of time. If you decide you're going to pay attention in college, there will be times when you will be overwhelmed by conflicting claims of truth, particularly if you attend a non-Christian college. And more to the point, your understanding and acceptance of God as the central reality in your life (the One you are trusting from the bottom of your heart) will most likely be mocked and ridiculed (more on this in the chapter about faith).

Integrity means you hold on to what you know is true even when you can't fully explain it or defend it. Someone wisely said that trusting God will sometimes mean we will continue to believe in the dark what we saw was true in the light. Integrity doesn't throw in the towel on truth just because a tenured professor or a powerful speaker declares there is no truth.

But the greatest challenges to your integrity will probably not come from outside. Your integrity will be questioned by that part of you that isn't all that sure, that wants to take an easier way, that wants to get along with everybody. There will be times when you will retreat into the silence of your mind and holding on to the truth will seem at that moment to be ridiculous. That's when you need to hear from God.

#3: Listen for God's voice in everything you do, everywhere you go.

The question included in the verse at the beginning of this chapter is perhaps as great a challenge to integrity as anyone has had to face. Job's wife's words have the same raw quality that we hear in Jesus' words from the cross: "My God, my God, why have you abandoned me?" Job's wife was distraught and grieving. She was angry at God and she was angry at her husband for continuing to trust God. God had just allowed most of her security to be destroyed or stolen. He had allowed her children to die. She had watched her husband break out in horrific, ugly, seeping boils. Now he was scratching himself on a heap of ash — gross. It's not all that surprising that she was at her wit's end. It doesn't take nearly that much to drive most of us crazy!

For all we know, Job was feeling exactly as his wife was. In the face of all the tragedy and overwhelming pain he was feeling, his "precious integrity" didn't seem all that impressive. But he didn't let his feelings have the last word. What was he doing? He was doing his best to listen for God's voice in everything he did and everywhere he went. Job had to wait for more than a week before God spoke to him. In the meantime, he had to endure his own grief and the accusations of several friends who just didn't get the point that bad things don't just happen to bad people. It wasn't that Job thought he was all that great a person, but he knew that God wasn't punishing him, so there had to be another explanation. In the end, God showed him that sometimes there's no explanation; there's just God. Ultimately, trusting God from the bottom of our hearts means trusting him beyond our understanding the answers.

We will probably not have to face the same kind of suffering that Job went through, yet life will stretch us to the limit. Our integrity will be tested. We'll learn whether or not we are willing to trust God.

#4: He's the one who will keep you on track.

Integrity relates to the bottom line in your life. When everything else is up for grabs, where will you turn? This time in your life is crucial because you are learning and establishing your life foundation. You are gathering some of the materials and learning the skills you will use throughout a lifetime. On your foundation, you will construct a life. Jesus used this exact picture to tell the crowds listening to him deliver the Sermon on the Mount what they were about to do with his words. He told them that they were really two groups: the sand builders and the rock builders.

> *These words I speak to you are not incidental additions to your life, homeowner improvements to your standard of living. They are foundational words, words to build a life on. If you work these words into your life, you are like a smart carpenter who built his house on solid rock. Rain poured down, the river flooded, a tornado hit — but nothing moved that house. It was fixed to the rock.*
>
> *But if you just use my words in Bible studies and don't work them into your life, you are like a stupid carpenter who built his house on the sandy beach. When a storm rolled in and the waves came up, it collapsed like a house of cards. (Matthew 7:24-27)*

We've come a long way from GPAs and credit scores, but the true measurement of life can be seen in the way Jesus' words have been built into someone's way of thinking and their way of acting. If you want to build a life that will withstand whatever storms life sends your way, make sure that Jesus' words are the structure and your relationship with him is your foundation.

BITES

"The little things we do or don't do make us who we are. Sometimes doing the right thing is not the easiest thing."

"Gossip only makes relationships depressing, and talking about how people gossip is gossip."

"College is no different than high school in this way: You still have to be thoughtful with what you're telling people and who you are talking about. If it's none of your business, leave it alone."

FAITH ON THE JOURNEY

Through thick and thin, keep your hearts at attention, in adoration before Christ, your Master. Be ready to speak up and tell anyone who asks why you're living the way you are, and always with the utmost courtesy.

1 PETER 3:15

The fact that you actually have a faith you intend to practice will be a surprise to many of the people you meet as you move away from home. When people leave home, they often quickly shed much of the "baggage" they brought with them. Forced or casual habits of faith are some of the first things to go. After all, they are now free — free from parental restrictions and possibly out from under any imposed restrictions that involved God. They are now operating under the mistaken notion that faith contradicts fun. They have decided that because faith will get in the way of fun, faith probably has to go (or at least be put in the closet for consideration later on).

For the time being, let's say that you're interested in both fun and faith. You don't see a contradiction between the two of them and suspect that living a life of genuine faith is the deepest kind of fun a human being can have. Faith keeps fun real and fun keeps faith grounded.

The place to start understanding this process of taking faith to school rather than leaving it behind is the life and ministry of Jesus. He began his work by gathering a class of twelve students that he called disciples. For the next three years, he enrolled them in a practical school of faith and ministry. They accomplished in three years what takes most college students four or more years because they were in class 24/7. Jesus taught on the move. There were many auditors in his classes, and all were welcome, but his primary instructions were for the twelve men he had chosen. Jesus did very little lecturing and a lot of show, tell, and do.

Jesus taught by example. The disciples watched him relate with every conceivable audience — from little children who were drawn to him to the elderly, sick, and dying. Crowds didn't flock to Jesus because he was serious; they flocked to him because he was so full of life! The people of Jesus' day had plenty of no-nonsense religious people around, but Jesus stood out, probably because he laughed a lot. The disciples were also witnesses to the tense encounters in which serious religious people criticized and attacked Jesus. His opponents were convinced he had too much fun and hung out with the wrong kind of people. Jesus handled them all in a truthful, firm, and loving way.

When you read the Gospels, remember how much Jesus was at home with himself in any surrounding. Wherever you go to college, Jesus would be comfortable there. People would be drawn to him. He would cause a stir. Who do you think would be upset by his presence? Would he be judged by some as entirely too religious? Would he be suspected by others as just too friendly with sinners? How would you feel hanging out with him?

The picture of Jesus in a modern setting reminds me of an incident I witnessed in a small country church several years ago. The singing in the service was lively, and people really seemed to be interested. Just before the sermon, the young pastor stood up and read the Scripture for the day. His passage was the episode in which Jesus met Matthew the tax collector and invited him to join his discipleship school. Matthew left his office and then invited all his friends to his house that night for a party to meet his new teacher. Jesus was criticized for keeping company with riffraff, but he responded by saying that these kinds of people were the very ones he came to save (see Matthew 9:9-13).

As the pastor was finishing his reading, a hand went up toward the back of the sanctuary. The motion caught his eye and he quickly said, "Yes. Is there a question?" As the words were leaving his mouth, I could tell that he suddenly realized that the hand that had been raised was connected to an arm that was connected to his teenage daughter. About a hundred curious faces turned toward the daughter. The pastor stood there with a nervous smile as his daughter rose to her feet and asked, "As you were reading what Jesus did and said in this passage, I couldn't help but wonder why our parents often try so hard to keep us from going to parties or hanging out with the wrong kind of people. Jesus spent a lot of time with sinners. Aren't we supposed to be like Jesus? Can you explain that?"

It was suddenly quiet in that church. A hundred heads turned back toward the pastor. I don't think people were breathing, especially the parents. The pastor later admitted that the first thing that happened was his mind went blank. He had been taken completely by surprise. He knew that this wasn't a trick question, but an answer was not apparent to him. He prayed, and when he opened his mouth, he actually sensed that God was giving him a wise answer that didn't come from his own thoughts. He smiled and said, "That's a great question, and I'm sure you're not the only one hanging on the answer . . . daughter." Lots of heads nodded and a few chuckled. He continued, "You're right. I believe that all of us as parents really want our kids to grow up as free as Jesus was and be able to relate with anyone. But there is something in this account of Jesus that we can't miss. These people wanted to be with Jesus. And they wanted to be like him. He didn't have to change or be different in any way, but when others were with him, they wanted to change their ways. What we as parents can often see is that our kids are too willing to change to be accepted by others. Jesus never compromised to be accepted by an audience. If we can see that our kids are confident in who they are in Christ, we are more likely to let them choose where they will go and with whom they will spend their time."

The daughter smiled and said, "Thanks . . . Dad!"

If your parents are believers, they are struggling with some of these feelings as they think about your going off to college. They wonder if your faith will survive. They've got good reasons to be concerned. Many people lose faith in college. Others come away so confused that their faith is permanently weakened. Yours doesn't have to be a victim of "higher" education. Asked what he wished someone had told him before he left home, one college student described the process this way:

Your faith will likely go through more changes in college than at any other time in your life. You might even believe completely differently than the way you were raised. What's most important about your faith journey at this time is thinking critically about what you really believe to be right and true and living accordingly instead of going with the flow of the environment around you.

If you go to a Christian school, don't take the easy way out and spout the same ideas as everyone else around you; if you go to a secular school, don't cave in to pressure and believe what everyone else does. Actually figure out who you are and why you have the faith you do. This is a process that lasts the rest of your life, but as soon as you start figuring

*things out, be true to that faith instead of merely
doing what's convenient.*

Because you don't really know yet exactly what challenges
your faith will face when you go away to school, the first wise
step is to identify what help and resources you will have while
on your own and devise a plan. In this chapter and the next,
we will be thinking about your plan. Here we will discuss the
on-campus aspects, and in the next chapter, we will look at the
off-campus aspects of your "faith that survives and thrives"
plan.

Depending on the size of the school you attend, you
might be amazed at the number of formal groups that meet
on campus for the purpose of offering spiritual growth from a
Christian perspective. Such groups as The Navigators, Campus
Crusade for Christ, and InterVarsity are three of the largest.
Your denomination might have staff that works on campus.
Ministries like these are *parachurch* (*para*-for, *church* — you
get the drift) groups. They serve as an extension of the church,
a special unit that represents the church in places where the
church may have limited access.

Every campus ministry seeks to be a well-rounded group
where Christian students can continue to grow spiritually while
they are in college and where non-Christian students can hear
and experience the truth of the good news about Jesus. But each
of these ministries functions under a unique philosophy and
approach. They have a particular emphasis or set of priorities
they carry out. These priorities give the groups a certain style

or tone. For example, historically The Navigators has emphasized healthy discipleship, Campus Crusade for Christ has focused on evangelism, and InterVarsity has emphasized the intellectual/scholarly side of Christianity. The effectiveness of any one of these groups on your campus may fluctuate depending on the staff, the history of the group, and the students who have chosen to affiliate with particular groups. Each campus ministry will usually offer a wide range of opportunities for spiritual growth ranging from occasional special events to regular large group and small group gatherings.

Typically, campus ministries will be under the direction of older, trained and professional staff. But the energy and day-to-day life of the ministry is often in the hands of students. Students often pass through a progression of experiences within campus ministries, beginning as observers, deciding to be attendees, growing into participants, and eventually joining in some kind of leadership capacity. Campus ministries are interactive and will usually be receptive to your interest and suggestions. Their view of ministry is to offer students not a prepackaged structure for involvement but a dynamic group experience in which the participants have a lot to do with the shape, tone, and life of the ministry.

So how do you make wise choices about the way you will express and grow your faith while in college? You are moving into a new situation, and by now you know that one tool you can use to think about an approach is the Choice Matrix.

#1: Trust God from the bottom of your heart.

There are plenty of people in your life who are praying and hoping that your college experience will include healthy spiritual growth. But beyond that group, God himself is committed to being with you, guiding you, protecting you, and growing you while you are in this transition time. When Jesus temporarily wrapped up direct physical ministry here on earth, he told his disciples (this was a kind of after-graduation party),

> *Go out and train everyone you meet, far and near,*
> *in this way of life, marking them by baptism in the*
> *threefold name: Father, Son, and Holy Spirit. Then*
> *instruct them in the practice of all I have commanded*
> *you. I'll be with you as you do this, day after day*
> *after day, right up to the end of the age. (Matthew*
> *28:19-20)*

Take a few moments to think about three phrases in this familiar passage: "far and near," "I'll be with you," and "day after day after day." The school you are entering may be geographically far or near to where you have lived up until now, but at times it will feel like the ends of the earth. If Jesus, who was about to ascend to heaven, could say to his disciples, "I'll be with you," then we can count on that promise today in the same way. We can't see him, but he is with us. The "far and near" and the "day after day" phrases tell us he is with us, as part three of the Choice Matrix indicates, everywhere we go.

What are some ways you can exercise trust in God as you

move into the world of college? He will be there whether you are alone or surrounded by crowds. You can count on him to guide you as you check out opportunities with the various campus ministries. Students are often amazed to discover how many other believers they can meet in a setting that doesn't officially promote Christianity and may in fact be openly hostile. Daniel and his friends, whom we met back in chapter 5, were certainly a minority at Babylon University, yet their small group made a huge impact. They didn't set out to create trouble or cause a scene, but when trouble came, they handled it in a way that brought glory to God. They trusted in God and stood together. As a result, they overcame a fiery furnace and a furious king (see Daniel 3).

Trust God to lead you to some faithful friends with whom you can face difficulties. You probably won't have to choose a trip into an actual roaring inferno, but opposition, ridicule, and misunderstanding can certainly turn up the heat on a campus. God's presence in your life means you can stand alone, but it doesn't mean that you are required to stand alone or that standing alone is somehow better than standing with other believers.

#2: Don't try to figure out everything on your own.

If you attend a secular campus, you might feel overwhelmed by the parade of religions and worldviews constantly on display. You may be impressed by the sincerity of the followers from other religions who approach you. The numbers will quickly convince you that you will never have time to figure them all out or know how to respond to each one. That's not your primary duty as a follower of Jesus anyway. People pursuing other faiths are simply trying to find what you have already found in Jesus. You need to be able to talk about the answer to life that you have found in such a way that when their search in other places comes up empty, they may remember what you said. One student noted,

> *I think that, even at a Christian school, it is easy to*
> *be judged based on what you believe or lack thereof.*
> *My advice is to know what you believe, think about it,*
> *recognize why you believe, and then be able to defend*
> *it. You will be put down, you will be argued with, but*
> *as long as you are comfortable with your decision*
> *and choices, it doesn't matter what other people are*
> *saying.*

Gathering with other believers on campus and listening to them talk about their faith will often help you think about the words you use and the way you communicate what you believe. Often we're unaware that we use vocabulary or expressions that are biblical but foreign to those who hear us. Biblical terms such as "saved," "redeemed," and "born again" may communicate clearly in context but often have a different effect in a world that is unaware of the context. Words such as "forgiveness," "acceptance," and "rescued" might strike a more responsive chord in people. Some people will relate to the following description of the Bible taken from Psalms: "By your words I can see where I'm going; they throw a beam of light on my dark path" (119:105). But you might get others thinking if you say, "The Bible is a combination of Mapquest and GPS that God has given to me."

Realize also that the greatest challenge to your faith will not likely come from other religions. That challenge will come from a worldview that dismisses Christianity (and all religion) as a part of a pluralistic curiosity, doubts the existence of absolutes, and tries to function in a closed, naturalistic system. This perspective proposes that we live in an accidental universe, we are the products of pure chance, and there is nothing and no one outside the system. The fact that this secular, naturalistic worldview is also a faith system seems to escape those who try to live by it.

You will hear a lot about tolerance. You might have to put up with obviously contradictory statements such as, "The only thing we won't tolerate is intolerance!" But the way you will tend to witness "tolerance" in practice will involve a combination of denying the truth claims of Christianity and defining all religions as equal in status because they are equally impotent. When you have to listen to versions of this in classes, the fact that Christianity has been anything but impotent in your life doesn't seem like much of a response, but it is. Developing relationships with other believers will provide you with constant reminders that the attempt to define Christianity as invalid is a lie designed to avoid the claims Jesus made. He has changed your life and other lives. Missionary E. Stanley Jones commented on the book he wrote explaining at length what Christ had done for him, "If what I've said in this book isn't true, it doesn't matter, but if it is true, then nothing else matters." The apostle Paul certainly knew his way around debates and presentations of theology, but he always came back to the basis of his faith with such statements as "I couldn't be more sure of my ground—the One I've trusted in can take care of what he's trusted me to do right to the end" (2 Timothy 1:12).

#3: Listen for God's voice in everything you do, everywhere you go.

Early on in this book, you read some brief comments about the book of Ecclesiastes. You should plan to read it several times while you are in college. You will be stunned that words written so long ago describe the spirit of this day. If you take out the crucial passages that acknowledge God in the book, Solomon's observations about life lived with nothing but the sun overhead reflect exactly the modern outlook: Life is meaningless. Only the bold and a few very popular authors will actually put it into words, but Solomon's conclusion is the contemporary discovery. Science, in trying to have the last word, has declared that everything is one long, drawn-out accident without meaning. But don't overlook your natural curiosity over why people who say they believe that life is meaningless would be going to such great lengths to convince all the rest of us that life is meaningless. The answer is because of something that Solomon also said. When people reject the truthful alternative to meaninglessness, they will do and say almost anything to keep their rebellion alive. What's being rejected? In Solomon's words, "Fear God. Do what he tells you" (Ecclesiastes 12:13). It's almost impossible to understand, but some people would rather consider life meaningless than fear God and do what he tells them.

Because you are applying the third phrase of the Choice Matrix and listening for God's voice everywhere you go and in everything you do, life is meaningful. You are letting God's Word speak into your life. If you seek out others on campus who are like-minded, you will be building an encouragement base that can help you along the way.

#4: He's the one who will keep you on track.

Life on campus will offer many official and informal settings where life issues will come up. Faith is always in the picture, but it isn't always recognized. Sometimes you will feel you've done well in explaining your faith; other times you will feel like you ended up with your foot in your mouth. This is all part of learning. Jesus is a lot bigger than your ability to explain or describe him. And it's not always about what you say. In fact, as we have discovered over and over, wisdom is seen when practice backs up and clarifies words. People will often "get" what you do and why you do it better than you can explain. Here's a reminder of the exciting thing: Effectiveness is ultimately not up to you. You can write a brilliant paper or present a logical explanation of the faith and discover that it went nowhere. You can walk away from a conversation convinced you confused someone else completely only to discover later that God spoke through you and altered that person's life eternally. That's just one way God will show you that he's keeping you and your faith on track with his plans.

BITES

"Stick to what you believe, but be open to listening to other people's opinions. If you have questions, ask someone who believes what you believe to help you understand."

"When sharing your faith, your words might be rejected. It is important not to be hostile in return. The best thing you can do is simply make a point for them to think about, not to win an argument."

"Your speech and actions should speak for themselves, but don't antici-pate that you can always be quiet about your faith. If people ask you, give them an honest answer. Prayerfully decide which topics and behav-iors you will take issue with, because careless words can damage your credibility in the future."

GETTING CONNECTED

Let's see how inventive we can be in encouraging love and helping out, not avoiding worshiping together as some do but spurring each other on, especially as we see the big Day approaching.

HEBREWS 10:25

M uch of the last chapter had to do with the way you carry out your life of faith in the context of those who might not be believers. The opportunity to gather with others on campus to study the Bible and encourage one another is one of the benefits of living in an academic community. There is something exhilarating about being with peers and motivating one another to excellence in knowing and serving Christ. Solomon included a proverb that gets at this idea: "You use steel to sharpen steel, and one friend sharpens another" (27:17). The quality of friendship determines the quality of sharpening. Make sure that you give attention to and work at relationships with your peers because they will eventually add to the qualities and growth in your life.

However, the school community of which you are a part will have two significant drawbacks that you need to account for in maintaining spiritual health and practicing wise living. The first of these is that the community is temporary. The second is that the community has a narrow breadth of experience and age.

In the previous chapter, we touched on how college years are a transition time. For how long you've lived, four years is a pretty long time. If you're eighteen, you are embarking on an experience equal to about a quarter of your life. But compared to your expected life span, these next four years will just be an intense parentheses. Keep in mind that while you are away at school, the rest of the world will not stop to wait for you. Life will continue to happen. You will be taking in all sorts of new and exciting ideas and experiences. But that doesn't mean that everyone at home is on freeze frame, waiting for you to stop by. The reason there's friction or disconnect when you visit isn't because so much has happened for you and nothing for them; it's because each of you has been moving on in life apart from the other. Reconnecting might not be easy.

For all its intensity, college lasts about four years. It's a bubble in time and a bubble in space. In many ways, your college campus will be a little society cut off from the rest of the world. You might do some travel abroad sponsored by your school, and that could be very beneficial, but the time you spend at school can more or less prepare you for the rest of life. But while you're getting educated, it's worth considering how you might stay engaged with the rest of life and other people, because before you know it, you'll have to leave school and rejoin the human race.

A college community has a narrow breadth of experience/age. The large majority of the students are within six years of age of one another. This limits the influence of older mentors and examples almost exclusively to professors. Now, professors, like all professions, may vary widely as to the quality of their wisdom and character, but the possible danger is that they represent a fairly narrow group to have a monopoly on your time and attention.

Meanwhile, the people you'll be living with are all your age, with approximately the same level of life experience. You'll be part of a group that can generate great energy but may have a severely limited capacity when it comes to understanding how things work. If you actually work at a job to support yourself and pay your bills while at school, that puts you in a different category of experience right away, particularly if you work off campus.

When asked what she would say to an incoming freshman about the place of church in the life of a college student, one upperclassman wrote, "Go to church! Go to one you enjoy. Make friends at church. Do church things with them. If I had known this, I am sure my struggles with faith would have been so much softer."

The church overcomes the temporariness of the college experience by keeping you involved with people of all ages who are living out their faith and facing their own challenges in life. Without even trying, the people at church will remind you that there's a much larger and longer culture outside the ivy-covered walls and that the knowledge that seems so all-encompassing in the classroom may not mean all that much on the streets two blocks from campus. One young man took advantage of an opportunity to lead a small youth group in church while he was in college. He wrote later that the weekly discipline of preparing to speak to those people who were only a few years younger than himself forced him to continuously choose between what was interesting but theoretical in school and what was practical: "I was supposed to lead those kinds and give them biblical instruction, but in exchange, they kept me grounded."

The church makes up for the limited breadth of experience available on campus by offering a wide range of life wisdom, some based on decades of making it work in the trenches. Each week, people from widely different walks of life gather under one roof to worship one Lord and Savior. You can join them and contribute your life to the whole. If what you are learning in school is really true and important, you need to pass it on to others. If what you are learning is simply something new and interesting but not particularly useful to anyone, then it has limited value where people really live. By spending time with people who are *not* in school, you are giving yourself a continual reminder of how the nonacademic world thinks and what they experience. You keep up with the language of people who are working in jobs and facing issues in life that you haven't yet had to deal with. In short, involvement in the church will give you a well-rounded life experience that will put everything you are learning in school into the context of reality.

There are a couple ways of thinking about the education you are about to receive related to the life you will live later on. One is the "fill then deliver" view, and the other is the "deliver as you fill" view. The "fill then deliver" approach means you are a container that must be completely filled up with knowledge before you can use any of it. This is a school-centered view that encourages you to step out of life in order to be fully prepared so you can then step back into life and deliver what has been poured into you. The "deliver as you fill" concept allows you to stay engaged with "outsiders" so that you discover along the way what is useful to others out of what you are learning. It's more a leaky bucket approach, where others get to benefit from what you are receiving shortly after you receive it.

You've probably practiced one of these two concepts regarding this book. You've either read this far privately or you have read to this point and discussed it with others along the way, letting others in on what you are learning and perhaps asking them questions about points along the way that don't seem clear. Your decision about the church while you are in school will follow the same pathway. This isn't about occasionally attending one or another church close to the college campus; this is about whether you will establish a church home away from home while you are in school. The "can't deliver until full" approach will allow you to pretty much check off the church for the next few years; the "deliver while filling" approach will allow you to have a significant relationship with a local church. This last approach will also certainly allow you to find out that some of the best "filling" you will receive along the way won't come from school but rather from what other believers pour into your life.

When it comes to our involvement in the body of Christ at any point in our lives, the phrases of the Choice Matrix can give us a road map for wise decisions.

#1: Trust God from the bottom of your heart.

The God you are trusting designed you for relationship with him and relationship with other believers. Most of the qualities God wants to grow in your life require that you be in contact with others who are also seeking to grow. God's plan becomes clear when you look at a basic description of church life, such as Ephesians 4:1-3:

> *In light of all this, here's what I want you to do. While I'm locked up here, a prisoner for the Master, I want you to get out there and walk—better yet, run!—on the road God called you to travel. I don't want any of you sitting around on your hands. I don't want anyone strolling off, down some path that goes nowhere. And mark that you do this with <u>humility</u> and <u>discipline</u>—not in fits and starts, but steadily, <u>pouring yourselves out for each other in acts of love</u>, alert at <u>noticing differences</u> and <u>quick at mending fences</u>. (emphasis added)*

Each of the underlined words indicates a positive trait God wants to develop in you, and each one requires other people in order to grow. Imagine for a minute working on humility all by yourself. It's easy, right? You can have a little conversation with yourself about ways you've become more humble. But put yourself in a room with two or more other people discussing almost any subject, and humility becomes a challenge in countless ways. Are you really listening to others? How do you respond when they don't listen to you or don't agree with what you suggest? What do you say when you don't agree with what they have said? Humility suddenly gets a lot harder. Then add the other areas Paul pointed out, such as pouring yourself out in acts of love for others, noticing when something is not right between you, and acting swiftly to mend fences with people. You could say that the church is the easiest place to really grow because it is so hard! That's because it's real growth instead of pretend growth. It isn't just you telling yourself that you are making good progress spiritually; it's about other people who really know you catching you by surprise and telling you, "I've been watching you and you have grown," or saying, "I was thinking the other day about people I know who really know how to serve others, and you definitely made my list!" Those statements aren't the kind of cheap encouragement we give ourselves. People are pointing out the real deal in us. And the best way to handle that is to make sure we are observing them and letting them know when we see progress in their lives.

Trusting God means that we accept his plan to grow us within his church, the body of Christ. It also means that we realize we are never going to find a local church that is perfect, because every one is made up of people like us who still have a long way to go. If we ever did find the perfect church, we wouldn't want to join it because our presence would immediately make it a not-so-perfect church. But we can find plenty of churches where we can grow and help other people grow. Choosing to find a local body of believers will be a significant application of wisdom as you make your way in college.

#2: Don't try to figure out everything on your own.

Avoid becoming a church sampler. When you're a college student or living on a tight budget, it's worth knowing what supermarkets in your neighborhood offer a lot of food samples. If you time it right, you can get almost a complete meal visiting the various booths that offer a taste of pizza, egg rolls, dips, chips—you know, the four food groups! But you don't want to approach your search for a church home that way. Be intentional and decisive. Have a plan.

For example, give yourself a couple of months to do church visits. Make a list ahead of time of some possibilities (close to campus or one that offers a shuttle for students, a denomination you are familiar with, a referral from older students you meet at campus ministry meetings, and so on). Check out the church websites to get a feel for the tone, know the schedule, and note anything about the way the church presents itself that provokes curiosity (they demonstrate an interest in college students, sponsor a special ministry you've wondered about, emphasize the Bible). Keep your list to about five churches at the most.

Once you've visited your list, decide on the one that most drew you. Have at least one clear reason why you want to visit that particular church again. When you've got a specific church in mind, visit it three weeks in a row and then make a decision. Commit to that church for the rest of the school year. Give that congregation and yourself some seasons to get to know each other.

It is important to ask questions about what a particular church has to offer you as a young person, but it is equally important to ponder what you have to offer them. If your only reason to commit to a church is because you like what it will do for you, you will tend to develop as a church sampler rather than a member of the body. When you are in school, you might not feel like you have a lot to time, but your connection with the body of Christ should be one of those commitments that remains a high priority. As one upper-class college student wrote,

> *View the church as a place to learn and grow and even as a place to just relax in your faith and the fellowship of other believers. Find a church you like and then force yourself to keep going even when you feel like just staying home and sleeping or working on homework. If you are in the right church, it will get easier to keep going because you will find out you really want to go, even if it means less sleep or less homework done.*
>
> *I encourage you to stick it out through times*

you might feel unmotivated to go to church, as it is wonderful when you come through and realize that you can still get everything important done and maintain your church relationships. You will appreciate having a place where there are people you love who love you and where you can completely escape from the stress of work, school, and sometimes just living.

Why you need the church or why the church needs you might not be something you can figure out completely at every moment. But in the course of life, your richest moments of service and greatest experiences of worship and learning will invariably be in the company of other believers in that mysterious bond called the church.

#3: Listen for God's voice in everything you do, everywhere you go.

Everything you've read so far in this chapter may have differed from your own church background. You might, in fact, think of going to church as a deeply painful or difficult experience. When you read that the church is filled with flawed people, perhaps you thought, *Yeah, and I have the scars to prove it!* Or you may simply feel as if you have had to endure years of Sundays with people who didn't seem to be in touch with the real world.

Yes, local churches are imperfect, and sometimes the imperfections run deep. Isn't it amazing how often people who are supposed to know better, and sometimes say they know better, do such hurtful things? But here you are, about to be on your own, having an opportunity to make wise choices about your life. Can you hear what God is saying to you about the scars from your past? He knows about all of it and wants to use even the hardest parts of your life and the most painful experiences with the church to create something wonderful for others.

You don't have to run from the hurts, and you don't have to assume that because you had a bad or even terrible church experience you can't find a healthy and whole fellowship that will live up to how God describes his body on earth. Consider this also: When someone is hurt in the context of the church, it isn't usually the congregation who creates the pain but an individual or a small group of people. There are often other wonderful people in that same congregation who would be stunned and dismayed if they knew how deeply someone else close to them had been wounded. You can probably identify some of those people. Those are the people you want to be like: people who do know Christ and live for him truthfully.

When you read the letters the apostle Paul wrote in the New Testament, note how often he mentions struggles, disappointments, and hurts—often from other believers. Yet he did not let those wounds keep him from loving the body of Christ. It's clear why. He remembered what it was like to be the one hurt and wounded. He was so amazed by the depths of God's forgiveness and acceptance that he didn't let the shortcomings of other Christians keep him from affirming the crucial role the body of Christ will always have in providing relationships in which people can grow spiritually.

It is possible to handle our disappointments with the church by staying away, but that's never a permanent solution. If we listen to God, we can begin to see those disappointments as experiences that will help us know how to make the experiences of other Christians better. The hurts, as deep as they might be, can give us a very special understanding of the hurts of others.

#4: He's the one who will keep you on track.

One of the opportunities that come with life on your own or away at school is the special part of independence that involves choosing your connections. Independence doesn't mean isolation; it means being responsible for initiating and keeping new relationships. When it comes to the church, it's unlikely that you decided what church your family would attend. Now's your chance to make your own decisions about which church is best for you. And even if, after college is over, you're planning to return to the church your family attends, you'll need to choose at least a temporary connection with the body of Christ.

Don't make a show out of this, but there is something deeply right about rising quietly on a Sunday morning and preparing to meet with others to worship the God who went so far out of his way to demonstrate how much he loves you. The rest of your dorm may be vibrating from the sounds of snoring, but there will be a particular sense of purpose in setting aside time to spend moments in God's presence and learn from his Word. Developing the habit will, in the long run, prove to be one of the significant choices that demonstrate maturity in your life.

WISE **BITES**

"Connect with a church. You just left your family. You need a new one.
This is where you will find it. And they need your talents!"

"Explore different churches and ways to worship instead of following
the (often forced) routine of your pre-college days."

"Go to church. There's no one to force you to go anymore, and if you
don't go on your own, you will end up missing it!"

10

THE WHO THAT I AM, REALLY

Indeed, I have been crucified with Christ. My ego is no longer central. It is no longer important that I appear righteous before you or have your good opinion, and I am no longer driven to impress God. Christ lives in me. The life you see me living is not "mine," but it is lived by faith in the Son of God, who loved me and gave himself for me. I am not going to go back on that.

GALATIANS 2:20

You can change, but you also can't. Strange, isn't it? You can grow, learn, and change a lot, yet you will still be you. You can never become someone else. Pretending only lasts so long. You are stuck with you — deal with it.

A couple of decades ago, the popular quest of young people leaving home was to "go find themselves." Usually that involved travel to a faraway place. Think about it for a minute. The story behind the phrase "Go find yourself" could be unfolded like this: Your self, like all selves, is really smart and practical, so it has gone to some exotic place like California or Colorado or even Europe. It is waiting there for you to come find it. Now, sometimes it plays hide-and-seek, so you might have to visit lots of exotic places in order to find your self. But if you're lucky, the script goes, you and your self will eventually meet up and live happily ever after.

The truth is that your self is in the very same seat where you are sitting. Your self shares some significant characteristics with your shadow. Your shadow is always there, and it only takes the right kind of light to see it. There's a significant and unavoidable truth in the old saying, "Wherever you go, there you are!"

Finding yourself has very little to do with going somewhere; it has more to do with finding the right light. The ancient Greeks had a saying that is closer to the truth: Know yourself. One of the discoveries you can get serious about at this point in your life is to identify the parts of you that are at the core. What makes you *you*? What will remain unchanged no matter how much you change? One of the best places to go to find ourselves, where the light is the best, is in God's Word.

When it comes to the issue of self, Christians have some difficulties keeping Scripture in balance. We get a little unclear about what the Bible tells us can change about us and what can't change about us. Here are a couple of passages that will help us see the importance of clarity:

You shaped me first inside, then out;
*   you formed me in my mother's womb.*
I thank you, High God—you're breathtaking!
*   Body and soul, I am marvelously made!*
*   I worship in adoration—what a creation!*
You know me inside and out,
*   you know every bone in my body;*
You know exactly how I was made, bit by bit,
*   how I was sculpted from nothing into something.*
Like an open book, you watched me grow from conception
*   to birth;*
*   all the stages of my life were spread out before you,*
The days of my life all prepared
*   before I'd even lived one day. (Psalm 139:13-16)*

We look inside, and what we see is that anyone united
with the Messiah gets a fresh start, is created new.
The old life is gone; a new life burgeons! Look at it!
(2 Corinthians 5:17)

The verses from Psalm 139 give us a great assurance that we were personally designed by God. Second Corinthians 5:17 is a verse that describes what appears to be a complete and radical makeover that happens when we are "united with the Messiah." But here's the thing that lots of people don't realize about God's radical spiritual makeover in our lives when we meet Jesus Christ: He changes us without changing us!

Psalm 139 describes God as an amazing artist who carefully

shapes and creates us in our mother's womb. One thing that is never, ever heard in God's workroom is "Oops!" God doesn't make mistakes. You might wonder why you are a certain way, and that "thing" may really bug you. The explanation that *won't* work for that part of you is that God wasn't paying attention the day he created you. You were custom-made. God fashioned you like no one else he has ever made. The only real downer to the whole process is that in conceiving you, your parents also passed on to you the human condition called sin. That means, as the Bible describes it, that you were physically born as God's unique creation but spiritually stillborn. You were born needing to be born again.

When 2 Corinthians 5:17 speaks about "a fresh start . . . created new," it is echoing the same simple picture Jesus used with Nicodemus in John 3 when he told the religious leader that even he must be "born from above" (verse 3). Neither Paul nor Jesus before him meant to say that being united with Christ would mean that God would have to recreate what he created in the first place. Both of them meant that the spiritual makeover that would take place would miraculously flood every nook and cranny of the original creation with new life but without really changing what God built into the person from the start. That's why your transformation by Christ means he has changed everything about you without changing you. And he is going to keep working on growing you into someone who is more and more like him without ever altering his original design.

You can trace how this works in the real people of the

Bible. God meets and transforms them, but you can still recognize them. An obvious example is Peter—the loud, impulsive, rough, courageous, big-hearted Peter. From the time Jesus called Peter away from fishing to the amazing days described in Acts when Peter preached sermons and then to the very end of his life when tradition tells us that Peter insisted the Romans crucify him upside down because he didn't want any comparisons between his death and that of Jesus, the disciple went through a lot of changes. He grew by leaps and bounds. He learned by listening and (mostly) by making mistakes. But he never stopped being Peter. All the characteristics God built in from the start—loudness, impulsiveness, roughness, courage, bigheartedness—God kept, controlled, and used for his purposes. God changed Peter by making him each day a better version of Peter than the day before without losing any of the original Peter he created back in Peter's mother's womb.

Now, that's God's plan for you. The transformation goes on, but you're still you. And your cooperation with God's purposes will have a lot to do with the choices you make along the way. This is a crucial area in which to apply the Choice Matrix.

#1: Trust God from the bottom of your heart.

God gave you the heart you get to use in trusting him. The first thing David wrote after describing God's personal involvement in his creation was "I thank you, High God—you're breathtaking!" (Psalm 139:13). Many of us are not likely to take that approach. We sound more like this: "Lord, you made me. I don't understand what you were thinking! There's my height, hair, eye color, coordination—need I say more? What about this 'handicap' I can't overcome? What about that 'thing' I have to deal with every day? No, I don't feel grateful. I'm holding you responsible, and sometimes I find myself getting really angry at you for making such a mess of me!" Sound familiar?

David's approach is not only better, it's wiser and healthier and gets us where we want to go much faster. It's almost impossible to feel good about ourselves while we are resentful of our Creator. But when we develop genuine gratitude to God for ourselves, even before we understand ourselves all that well, we can feel good about ourselves. We are personally autographed originals: valued, priceless, and with a purpose behind our design and creation. If you've never prayed a prayer like the following, it would be an excellent way to begin not only your life on your own but also your inner journey of self-discovery.

Lord, thanks for making me me. There's plenty I still don't understand about myself, and some of it I may never figure out, but I want to express my trust in you by telling you thanks for making me just as I am. As David said, you personally put me together, and I believe you did it with certain plans and purposes in mind. Help me to be attentive to the ways you want to teach me about myself so that I can not only trust you but also serve you from the bottom of my heart.

#2: Don't try to figure out everything on your own.

You might live a great deal of your life without understanding why God made you a certain way. In fact, you may not discover until you reach heaven how he worked through you in a certain unique way even though you never figured it out. Sometimes trusting God really has to take over when we're frustrated that we can't figure things out on our own. Paul commented on this when he wrote, "We don't yet see things clearly. We're squinting in a fog, peering through a mist. But it won't be long before the weather clears and the sun shines bright! We'll see it all then, see it all as clearly as God sees us, knowing him directly just as he knows us!" (1 Corinthians 13:12). Someday we won't have to try to figure things out anymore — we'll know.

In the meantime, we need help in discovering who we are. If God hardwired us as his unique creations, the life we have already lived contains clues about our basic makeup. So it doesn't hurt to ask the people who have watched us our whole lives what strengths and tendencies they have noticed in us. Ask them, "When you imagine me out ten or fifteen years from now, what do you see me doing?" They might share their dreams for you, but they might also give you some startling insights into patterns in your life that stood out for them that you didn't realize were so obvious.

You can make progress in identifying your uniqueness by determining what categories you fit into in certain areas. For example, people tend to fit primarily into one of three categories when it comes to functioning with other people: Some are individualists, some are team players, and some are supervisors. You probably have a little experience trying each of those functions, but one of them will be your primary default preference. If you are an individualist, you prefer to work alone, even when you are working with and for other people. No matter what the task, you want to know and do your specific part. If you are a team player, you don't want to work alone and you aren't necessarily interested in identifying exactly your part. You can pitch in here and there and not really care as long as the thing gets done. When you face a task, your first question may be *Who will work with me to do this?* If you are a supervisor, you know how to get work done without having to always touch it yourself. You primarily work through other people.

All these roles are significant and essential. Most tasks get done because a combination of these roles has been carried out. The fact that you are holding a book in your hand right now is proof that individualists, team players, and supervisors all did their work.

Another basic area worth clarifying is your love style. One book that will be of great help to you is *The Five Love Languages*, by Gary Chapman (Moody Publishers). In a similar way to the way we work with people, we experience and express love in five different ways. These are, Chapman explains, like languages. One is primary to us even though, like language, we can learn to "speak" the other four languages. But one of them will be our "native" language. These five languages can be summarized as expressing/experiencing love through words, touch, gifts, service, and time. If you were ever showing love like crazy to someone and they just weren't getting it, one explanation is that they didn't "speak" the same love language you use. Once you identify your love language and work at identifying the love languages of the people around you, you will be amazed at the difference that will make in the quality of your relationships.

People (particularly women who tend to think relationally anyway) can read the list of love languages and instantly identify theirs. Remember that you are surrounded by people "speaking" other love languages. You only have a one in five chance of having the same love language as the person you marry. Even if you do have the same love language, there will still be subtle, unique differences that you can take real delight in learning.

The traits and approaches you've just been reading play a role in your life every day, whether you are aware of them or not. Becoming aware of them is a huge step in discovering who you are. God and others can help you see it.

#3: Listen for God's voice in everything you do, everywhere you go.

In preparing this book, a number of graduating college students were asked to reflect on what they wished someone had talked to them about before they went to college. You have been hearing from them throughout. Their comments on self-discovery were particularly telling in that they were sharing what God has been teaching them about the way he made them. Starting college with that knowledge will put you several steps ahead. Listen for God's voice through their experiences.

One student wrote,

> *Take some time to think seriously about your relation-*
> *ship with God and who he has called you to be. This*
> *is different from what he has called you to do. How*
> *does your present life fall short of that? Why will you*
> *do those things? How can you start doing them now?*
> *How do you think you could be different in ten years?*
> *You will become the person you believe yourself to be.*
> *Know who God has called you to be and start acting*
> *that way.*

This student has learned that more attention needs to be given to a person's wiring and motivation rather than career choices and types of work. You may end up doing lots of different work in many different roles, but God has called you to be only one person: you.

Another student wrote,

> *Don't do anything simply because people around*
> *you are doing it or other people are telling you*
> *what is right. One big thing I didn't realize was that*
> *in college, consequences were a lot more serious*
> *and long-lasting than they were when I was a kid.*
> *However, don't dwell on past mistakes, but deter-*
> *mine to learn from them and be the best person*
> *you can possibly be. Try to discover why you are*
> *the way you are, and think critically about the way*

you were raised, the personality you have, and any
other factors that affect your lifestyle at the present
moment. I strongly suggest asking Dr. Phil's question
"Is it working for you?" If you don't like who you are,
figure out what you have to change and how to go
about doing that. Most important, embrace who you
are to the best of your ability.

Note in this student's discoveries the lesson that the consequences of mistakes have a greater impact the older you get.
This comes with the expanded responsibilities you are gain-
ing. Look for opportunities to practice what you are discovering
about yourself. You might be able to find these within both the
church you're attending and campus ministries.

Another college student noted,

You will not figure yourself out in the next four years.
The best you're going to get is a more solid idea of
where you're headed. To help find out where you're
going, approach conversations with an open mind
and defenses down. Most important, pray for wisdom.
Never stop praying for wisdom. It is the best skill you
can have to help other people, excel in college, and
take advantage of opportunities. But be warned: If
you pray for it, God will give it to you. Make sure you
understand what you're asking for (in other words, hit
Ecclesiastes and Proverbs).

The heart of this student's counsel is to direct you back to continually listening for God's voice. God designed you and he also designed life's systems. The way you can best operate within the systems that God has designed involves wisdom—living skillfully. There is nothing more satisfying than discovering opportunities where you are functioning in sync with God's plans and using the best you have in his service.

#4: He's the one who will keep you on track.

We began this chapter with the idea of finding or knowing yourself. This is a great task God has before you, and it is part of fulfilling your design. He created you and has every intention of working through you to bring about his plans. God did not create in you a simple equation or an elementary puzzle that can be figured out in a few moments. The you he designed will take a lifetime to unfold, discover, and implement. Realize that you are surrounded by people who are equally complex in whom God has also invested not only his creative efforts but also the very life of his Son in sacrifice. What you now know about God's design places a responsibility on you to never treat others as somehow inferior. Don't ever consider yourself inferior either. Humility isn't devaluing ourselves; it's joyfully finding our value in the One who made us and then made us again without altering all the wonderful original work he did on us. Recognizing where you came from and whose personal signature you bear will keep you on track throughout life.

WISE BITES

"If there is ever a time to struggle with the questions of 'Who am I?' and 'Why am I this way?' college is that time. That is all you can do. Ask the questions and work through them. Don't give up on the process."

"It's okay to ask tough questions. The Bible has nothing against it. But make sure that behind your questions is the honest desire to know God and not anger or spite."

"This is your time to explore who you are and who you want to be without becoming exactly like your parents. Ask yourself things about what you really want and what you really like to do. Find out who you are, and be open to things you might never have considered before."

"Do ask hard questions and challenge yourself, but don't be afraid to let the answers come slowly."

11

THE VALUE OF FREE TIME

There's an opportune time to do things, a right time for everything on the earth.

ECCLESIASTES 3:1

The bags are packed in the car. Your room is still your room, but there's less of you there. The wide world is waiting. And suddenly your time is your own — or so it seems.

Leaving home is like starting your own time clock. The feeling can hit you in many ways. You may feel as though the gun just went off in a race to freedom. You are sprinting to take it all in. Or you may heave a deep sigh and realize you now have a chance to set your own pace in life. You get to be the one to tell you what to do. You might even be feeling like you just crossed (or are about to cross) a finish line and you just want to take a few breaths before you start running again. You are now on your own time.

At this point, a reality check is in order. You do understand that the time clock is not guaranteed to keep running, right? In fact, depending on how many people read this book, there's a definite chance that someone reading these words has only a few days left on their time clock. If it's you, you probably don't know it. If you did know you had only limited time, would it affect your decisions? How? The point of living wisely ultimately is to live in such a way that it really doesn't make that much of a difference whether we die today or many years from now. The activities might be different, but the reasons for doing whatever we are doing are the same. They are the purposes worth doing no matter how long we live.

A young pastor stood before his congregation and said, "One of my duties as your pastor is to show you how God's Word can help you live very well. Another of those duties is to prepare you to die very well. I've found that people who understand how to die well also know how to live well." Stillness settled over the sanctuary. The people gathered seemed to be breathing slowly as one. They were listening intently.

He continued, "As I look out over this sanctuary, I'm struck by the number of vivid memories I have of people sitting in certain places that are now vacant or occupied by someone else. I've buried a few people who have been part of our lives together, and I must tell you that in saying temporary farewells to those brothers and sisters, in preparing for those funerals, and in talking with grieving families, I've become convinced that we don't talk enough about living and dying well. Today I want to introduce you to what I think is an exciting little quest that can have a huge impact in the way we live. I want to encourage you to begin seeking a life verse."

The concept of a life verse isn't new, and it has probably been applied by people throughout history using other terminology. The idea is to keep your mind and heart open for a passage from Scripture that uniquely summarizes your understanding of your relationship with God. A life verse becomes almost like a spiritual fingerprint that characterizes that person's life. It becomes an accountability expression for people to use to check their spiritual progress—how they're living up to their life verse. Here's an excellent example that many young people have used as an interim life verse while they were seeking their own: "Don't let anyone put you down because you're young. Teach believers with your life: by word, by demeanor, by love, by faith, by integrity" (1 Timothy 4:12). First, the verse connects with where you are in life right now: young. Second, the verse gives you a lot to work on: five specific areas where you can teach by example the your actions, love, faith, integrity, and words. Third, the verse provides a great checklist for self-evaluation. Your performance in any situation can be examined using those five areas.

Let's say you go home for a weekend with mixed results. You return to school and you're not really sure exactly what wasn't quite right, but you want to take responsibility for living as a growing follower of Jesus, especially when you are with your family. Here are some 1 Timothy 4:12 questions:

- In what ways did my speech patterns and language convey respect, genuine interest, and value to my family? What terms caused hurt or provoked arguments? Did I really need to say those things? Why?
- How did my demeanor and actions affect the weekend? Did I act adult-like or did I revert to some childish behavior? Did I pitch in with household duties and serve other family members cheerfully, or did I assume they should take care of me?
- In what obvious and subtle ways did I express love for my family while I was home? How do I know they got the message? How might I communicate love more clearly the next time?
- How did I convey to my family that I'm growing in my faith? Did I bring it up or did they have to ask? If they asked, were their questions based on positive changes they noticed in me or based on their concerns and lack of comment from me?
- How would I describe my level of integrity with my family this weekend? Did I give them a true picture of my life away from home, or did I keep a lot hidden that I don't want to have to explain? Did I respond to their questions openly or defensively?

A life verse can function like a screen saver on your mental monitor, a part of God's Word that you know you can work on in some way every day. Putting your life verse into action is a great way to spend any day, even your last.

If the only result of reading this book is that you identified and began to meditate on a life verse, your time will have been well spent. Ask God to keep you alert and lead you to a corner of his Word that can be your own. You will be amazed when you discover that passage how it expresses your heart and soul.

One young man from the pastor's church mentioned before took his challenge seriously. A little while later, he was reading in the Psalms and stopped at 94:17, "If God hadn't been there for me, I never would have made it." He looked it up in several different Bible versions and finally memorized it as, "If the LORD had not been my help, my soul would soon have lived in the land of silence" (ESV). When he showed his life verse to his pastor, who also happened to be his dad, the pastor was a little puzzled, but he thanked his son for following through on his invitation. At first he thought the boy might have just chosen the first verse that looked good. But the more he meditated on the verse, the more he realized that it perfectly expressed not only his son's personality but also his son's deepest understanding of his own relationship with God. The key phrase that spoke to his son was "land of silence." Those words described the boy's inner frustration with communication and his difficulty in putting ideas into words. In the Hebrew language, the phrase "land of silence" is one way to describe death. But this boy also understood it as a kind of silence even before death that makes a person closed off to everything and everybody. He wanted to participate in life fully and was learning that without God's help every day, he was going to die a little. In the years that have followed, his father has watched his son's life verse come true in all the ways God has been his help and the fact that he lives nowhere near the land of silence.

#1: Trust God from the bottom of your heart.

Here's an amazing fact: All time is free. Often the term *free time* is used to talk about moments that haven't been committed to a specific purpose, but in truth, every moment is free. Each second is a gift. We could spend every second saying thanks for the previous second of life. Fortunately, God accepts an attitude of gratefulness without insisting that we specifically name each item for which we are thankful because there are many more than we have time to count or mention.

God's Word includes some powerful commentary on time that is worth keeping in mind. Here's a poetic reflection on the impact of time on life:

There's an opportune time to do things, a right time for everything on the earth:

A right time for birth and another for death,
A right time to plant and another to reap,
A right time to kill and another to heal,
A right time to destroy and another to construct,
A right time to cry and another to laugh,
A right time to lament and another to cheer,
A right time to make love and another to abstain,

A right time to embrace and another to part,
A right time to search and another to count your
     losses,
A right time to hold on and another to let go,
A right time to rip out and another to mend,
A right time to shut up and another to speak up,
A right time to love and another to hate,
A right time to wage war and another to make
     peace. (Ecclesiastes 3:1-8)

Believe it or not, a band called The Byrds (they were popular in the shadow of the Beatles) had a huge hit with these verses put to music by Pete Seger. You could find it easily online. The song was called "Turn, Turn, Turn," and people could hardly believe the lyrics came directly from the Bible. Then again, when the Bible gets a chance, it constantly amazes people by the way it nails the issues of life. There *is* a right time for many things in life, and we don't want to miss them.

As you move out on your own, one of your privileges is going to be the freedom to assign much more of your time based on your choices. You will have to decide every day how to use the time God gives you that day. And whether you realize it or not, you will have to recognize many of the "times" mentioned in Ecclesiastes and do your best to live them fully.

Often we assume we can use time the way we want. Instead, we must recognize that certain opportunities come at certain times and if we miss the time, we miss the opportunity. You can see how this works in your experiences in your family over the last few years. There are probably several things your parents wished they had gotten around to doing with you that never worked out. There was a right time to do those activities or have that conversation, but now that time is almost over, and with it the opportunity. The "right time" to parent is when your kids are kids. If you wait until they grow up and then say, "Okay, I've decided I'm now ready to do some parenting. I was too busy years ago, but now I've got the time." The reality is that you have the time but it's no longer the right time.

The principle of "right times" in verses in Ecclesiastes will be proven over and over for you while you are in college. You'll have to discover the difference between "a right time to study" and "a right time to hang out and play video games." People who never learn to identify "right times" are people who have a hard time getting anything done.

You are now on a learning curve about the use of time. Hopefully you've already got some lessons under your belt that you can put to good use. You can probably agree that your degree of academic success in high school has had a lot to do with how well you budgeted time. In one of David's psalms, he included a thought that can serve as an excellent daily prayer for you as you manage God's gift of time: "Hour by hour I place my days in your hand, safe from the hands out to get me" (Psalm 31:15). The English Standard Version of this verse is, "My times are in your hand." We can trust God to help us manage the time he gives us.

People often forget that Moses wrote a prayer that is part of the collection called Psalms in which he connected God and time. He included a thought parallel to David's when it comes to being aware of God's role in the way we use time: "Oh! Teach us to live well! Teach us to live wisely and well!" (Psalm 90:12). The classic King James Version of this verse is, "Teach *us* to number our days, that we may apply *our* hearts unto wisdom." "Number our days" doesn't just mean keeping track of the calendar or counting down the days until graduation. It means having a growing appreciation for the opportunities to grow and learn that each day presents; it means not letting days slip by, but seeking to honor God with the way we use his gift of time. It means trusting God to lead us into wisdom.

#2: Don't try to figure out everything on your own.

There's an important difference between being aware and wise about time on the one hand and getting worried about time on the other. It's easy to start thinking, *I'm never going to have enough time to do everything that has to be done and everything I want to do!* Don't worry, because you are exactly right. There *will* be more to do than you can get done, even if you handle your time perfectly. If you know this from the start, you won't be surprised when it comes true. But worrying about not having enough time is certainly a waste of time. The people who learn not to worry about what they won't get done actually get a lot more done than those who waste part of the time they do have fretting over the time they don't have.

Jesus has also weighed in on time, and he warned about worrying about it. He has some helpful guidelines about how to handle worry and how to establish priorities. Using priorities means learning to line up the things we know need to get done each day and getting to them rather than spending time on things that can wait. As you think about time, you will want to return to Jesus' words often:

If you decide for God, living a life of God-worship, it follows that you don't fuss about what's on the table at mealtimes or whether the clothes in your closet are in fashion. There is far more to your life than the food you put in your stomach, more to your outer appearance than the clothes you hang on your body. Look at the birds, free and unfettered, not tied down to a job description, careless in the care of God. And you count far more to him than birds.

Has anyone by fussing in front of the mirror ever gotten taller by so much as an inch? All this time and money wasted on fashion—do you think it makes that much difference? Instead of looking at the fashions, walk out into the fields and look at the wildflowers. They never primp or shop, but have you ever seen color and design quite like it? The ten best-dressed men and women in the country look shabby alongside them.

If God gives such attention to the appearance of wildflowers—most of which are never even seen—don't you think he'll attend to you, take pride in you, do his best for you? What I'm trying to do here is to get you to relax, to not be so preoccupied with getting, *so you can respond to God's* giving. *People who don't know God and the way he works fuss over these things, but you know both God and how he works. Steep your life in God-reality, God-initiative, God-provisions. Don't worry about missing out. You'll find all your everyday human concerns will be met.*

Give your entire attention to what God is doing right now, and don't get worked up about what may or may not happen tomorrow. God will help you deal with whatever hard things come up when the time comes. (Matthew 6:25-34)

You don't have to figure out everything about time before you decide not to worry about it.

#3: Listen for God's voice in everything you do, everywhere you go.

When you read about the lives of people who have made an impact for God, one of the characteristics they seem to share is their attentiveness to God. No matter what they were involved in at the moment, God was on their minds. They were engaged with life but keenly aware of Life. They carried a heavy weight of responsibilities and admitted their weakness, but they counted on strength beyond and below them to carry the real weight. Paul wrote,

Actually, I don't have a sense of needing anything personally. I've learned by now to be quite content

whatever my circumstances. I'm just as happy with
little as with much, with much as with little. I've found
the recipe for being happy whether full or hungry,
hands full or hands empty. Whatever I have, wherever
I am, I can make it through anything in the One who
makes me who I am. (Philippians 4:11-13)

These qualities of attentiveness and contentment are not instinctive; they are learned. Paul wrote, "I've learned by now" and "I've found," meaning he didn't reach that kind of maturity overnight.

As we have discovered repeatedly throughout these chapters on wise living, the presence of God's Word in our hearts and minds forms the spiritual podcast we've downloaded into our mental iPods for continual play. Time spent learning and thinking about God's Word will give back rich dividends of contentment and lead you into wise choices.

#4: He's the one who will keep you on track.

Given the subject of this chapter, the final phase of the Choice Matrix could be expressed, "He's the one who will keep you on time." One of the verses from Psalm 139 that we looked at in the last chapter states,

Like an open book, you watched me grow from concep-
tion to birth;
all the stages of my life were spread out before you,

The days of my life all prepared
before I'd even lived one day. (verse 16)

Seek to live your life with an awareness that you are part of God's plan and that he has his hand on your life. Your shortcomings, glitches, failures, and wandering along the way are not going to surprise him or derail his plans. The more you take the time to practice trusting him, the more you will have that vivid sense that your life really is on track—on his tracks.

BITES

"Make good choices. Decide what is important to you and spend your time in a manner that reflects those values. Do your homework, on time."

"I wish someone would have told me that my best times in college would be spent lying on a couch talking, just talking. Oh, and making fun friends."

"Hang out with friends. Try to balance work and play so that you can do well in your studies but still create friendships that could last years."

THE MYSTERIES OF MONEY

Lust for money brings trouble and nothing but trouble. Going down that path,
some lose their footing in the faith completely and live to regret it
bitterly ever after.

1 TIMOTHY 6:10

F or many young people, the decision to go to college triggers
the most intense discussion about money they have ever had
with their parents. If you are fortunate, you've been learning a
little bit about money management while you've been in high
school. If not, you might be in a little bit of a panic. You will
survive, but it's important to get serious about money.

Hopefully you've had some part-time jobs and earned some
money. If you've developed the earn it/spend it approach to

finances, you need to step up for some significant lessons on the way money works and how to keep it from becoming the center of life.

Families take very different approaches to the financial part of their children going off to college. You might have parents who have saved money for you to go to college or have the financial resources to provide college for you. If you haven't been deeply grateful for the opportunity, it's time to start saying, "Thanks!" in a big way. There's no law that says your parents have to pay for college or even help you go. They may have told you you're on your own or that they would love to help but are financially strapped themselves and can't provide help. They might decide to take out loans to help you or arrange for you to take out government-backed loans. Don't assume that your family will automatically make finances easy for you. You may have to make some very hard decisions about money for the first time in your life.

Here are a few thoughts from a college student:

*Depending on your situation, it is now your respon-
sibility to take care of any bills, loans, and credit
cards you have. Getting a job is a good idea, even if
you hate it. Without your parents around, you will
discover that everything costs a whole lot more than
you ever thought.*

The mystery of money is the way money seems hard to talk about. But realize there's a lot of good and wise information about money out there and easy to access. Of course, you have to take the time and pay attention. First, the Bible provides you with a wealth of practical counsel on the place and use of money. Several specialized ministries have been developed to help people learn the truth about money. If just thinking about money makes you feel overwhelmed, enroll in a program of self-education. Go online and check out some of the following websites: www.crown.org, www.focusonthefamily.com (click "Life Challenges" and then choose "Managing Money"), www.masteryourmoney.com, www.navpress.com (do a keyword search on money), and www.wiserwoman.org. There's even a government site (www.mymoney.gov) that gives general basic information on finances. The Dave Ramsey show on many radio stations provides solid financial counsel and wisdom that has long been ignored in our culture.

Before you take out loans for college or start living on your own, talk to some people who are already doing it. Ask people who are a school year ahead of you what they have learned living out on their own. They can at least give you some warnings of what's to come. If you have lived at home without any financial responsibilities, you are not prepared for the financial part of living on your own, no matter how ready you feel to leave the house. The emotional need for freedom is going to take a hard hit from the reality of poverty.

Briefly, there are four guidelines that can keep you out of financial trouble. These can also show you that you are not as prepared as you might have thought for living on your own. They are:

- Spend less than you earn. That means that if you are not earning anything, you shouldn't be spending anything. If you are spending but not earning, you are spending someone else's money.

- Avoid using debt. Money you borrow is *always* easier to spend than to pay back, especially if it grows through interest (what banks and credit cards charge you to use their money).

- Set aside money for emergency purposes. This is part of what you do with the money left over when you are spending less than you are earning.

- Develop some long-term habits and plans for your financial future. If you can't learn to save, give, and budget when you have a little income, you won't find it any easier to do these things when you are making more money. Bad habits will set in that will be hard to break.

If your parents have a hard time talking to you about money, go to your pastor and ask who he or she would recommend you talk to for some wise financial counsel. Pastors usually know who in their congregations have a healthy perspective on money, and yours might be able to arrange an appointment with someone who can give you basic guidance.

Halfway through this book, we discussed integrity and the importance of keeping commitments. Remember that taking out a loan and even using a credit card involves a promise to pay back what you borrowed. You've given your word. Not paying your debts in a timely fashion can put a huge stain on your reputation. It calls into question your trustworthiness.

Money is or will be a significant part of your life. It's important to recognize it clearly for what it is without giving it more control or significance in your life than it deserves. Continue to apply the wisdom of the Choice Matrix as you learn to deal with money.

#1: Trust God from the bottom of your heart.

In some ways, it's a little funny that we write the words "In God we trust" on our money. The words remind us of a constant temptation we have to trust in the money rather than the God it mentions as worthy of trust. Written on every dollar bill is God's reminder of the way he keeps this promise: "No test or temptation that comes your way is beyond the course of what others have had to face. All you need to remember is that God will never let you down; he'll never let you be pushed past your limit; he'll always be there to help you come through it" (1 Corinthians 10:13). So when those tempting bills float through our hands, each has a little billboard that lets us know that the paper is not worth trusting like we can trust God.

If you and your parents have saved money all along with college in mind, putting that money to its intended use isn't that hard a decision to make. But if there is no money available, the decision whether or not to incur debt for schooling is a matter to consider seriously before God. The fact is that providing funds is one of the means God has at his disposal for guiding us. If there is no money available, God may be indicating that our original plan has to be put on hold. For a long time, loan money has been so available in our society that God's ability to guide by withholding funds has been easily ignored. If we refuse to at least consider that the money isn't there because God wants us to think again, we run the risk of making rash decisions that are going to lead us into further or difficult debt. When it comes to borrowing for education, one factor might be the degree to which the student has an established plan for school that will lead to a particular career that would provide funds for rapid repayment of the borrowed money. For example, someone who has a passion for education and wants to train to be a teacher might consider a school loan for that purpose. But someone who simply wants to experience college and doesn't have a particular end in mind might think twice about going into debt for such an approach.

Something even easier to trust than God or money is a credit card. At least with money you are handing over the bills. That makes a difference. Financial advisors can prove mathematically that people using credit cards will typically spend significantly more than people using cash. Handing over plastic doesn't feel as though you are really spending. This factor is why advisors will often train people to budget by using something like an envelope system, where the cash is assigned to envelopes labeled food, rent, insurance, entertainment, loan payment, and so on. Money in those envelopes can be used only for those purposes. If the food envelope is empty, time to tighten the belt. Credit cards let you pretend to put off payment into the future, but they make the payment more difficult. People making the minimum payments on their credit cards often don't realize they are doing the exact opposite of the first step of wise financial management. Instead of spending less than they earn each month, they are spending more than they earn each month and digging themselves into a debt hole. The hard-and-fast rule for responsible credit card use is this: If you can't pay off the full statement when it comes each month, you shouldn't be using the card. If and when you get a credit card, make the commitment that the first time you are unable to make the full payment, you will cease to use that card, or any other card. One college student reported some hard-learned wisdom about using credit cards:

> *There are only two reasons you could possibly need a credit card in college: emergencies and building credit. Don't get a credit card until your senior year, and then use it only for groceries once or twice a month. Pay it off in full. I know that sounds crazy, but college students do not know how to save and spend. Get a job, work ten to twenty hours a week, and learn to spend only less than the money you earn. Once you have a handle on boundaries and budgets, along with a healthy fear of being broke, then you can get a credit card.*

Living within your means is actually an exciting experiment in trusting God with your whole heart. If you fall back on debt anytime there seems to be a tight period coming, you will regularly miss out on God's supplying in very special and surprising ways to those who trust him.

#2: Don't try to figure out everything on your own.

By now you realize that God uses not only his Word but also other Christians to help us figure things out. People who get into financial problems are often people who tried to figure things out on their own or who took advice from people they had no reason to trust. If someone's financial advice includes selling you something, make sure you get a second opinion on the value of what is being offered. When an offer related to finances seems too good to be true, it most likely is. Recently in the news, there have been stories (the Madoff one is particularly shocking) about smart people having been taken for billions of dollars.

#3: Listen for God's voice in everything you do, everywhere you go.

Trusting God for our income is one thing; practicing trust in God with our spending is another. The area of giving is a particular area in which many Christians have unclear thinking or bad habits when it comes to money. If we don't live within our means, we won't have money to give to help others. One of the clearest ways we experience the freedom of not trusting money too much is by giving some of it away. Giving doesn't just supply funds to help other people and keep the church lights on; it benefits the giver. The act is a way of saying to God, "I'm trusting you to keep meeting my needs by not withholding what I can do for others. I'm giving as an act of thanksgiving for what you have given to me, Lord."

The tithe is no longer a rigid rule, but it is a very practical and easy way to track our giving habits. A tithe (tenth) is easy to figure in your head. If you make a hundred dollars, one-tenth of that can be joyfully given to God. The percentage approach allows you easy transition from one level of income to the next. The tithe is consistent, but the amount increases as income increases. Being faithful when the amount is relatively small makes it easier to be faithful when the amount becomes relatively large. But the giving is actually the same. The act of tithing is a specific opportunity to discover how God takes care of those who seek to be faithful. People who are tithers find their needs met. They discover they can't out-give God. Your experiment with tithing doesn't have to be public. Just make a commitment that the first 10 percent of the funds God provides you will be given back to him. See what happens. Track the results—the blessings God brings into your life. You will discover that it is actually fun to practice trusting God.

The kind of life that doesn't hold on to money too tightly honors the counsel God gives in passages such as this one in Hebrews: "Don't be obsessed with getting more material things. Be relaxed with what you have. Since God assured us, 'I'll never let you down, never walk off and leave you'" (13:5).

#4: He's the one who will keep you on track.

Money is a physical thing, and that makes it an obvious tool for teaching lessons and making points. As long as we insist on using money as one of the resources we can place before God for use in the world, we won't run the danger of trusting it more than we trust God. Electronic funds are less "real," but they can certainly exert a strong hold. Ask someone who had money invested in the market when it lost so much value at the end of

2008 and the beginning of 2009. What was worth sixty thousand one day was worth forty thousand the next. People looking at that drop received a golden opportunity to experience at an emotional level where their trust was really resting. If their trust was in the numbers, they experienced a financial disaster, but if their ultimate trust was in God, who knows and governs all things, the rapid number change was a little setback that means little in the huge scope of what God can do.

This fourth phase of the Choice Matrix is always a forward look, a trusting view of the future. We begin declaring that we are trusting God from the bottom of our hearts today, this moment. But as we work through the Choice Matrix with the subject matter we are considering, we are invited to look into the days to come. The lessons we apply today prove effective, so we plan to use them again tomorrow. The things we discover about God in the light of today we decide will continue tomorrow even if things seem darker. Wisdom is ultimately about trusting God and living the adventurous life he planned for you.

WISE BITES

"Moderation is key; budgeting helps."

"Get an internship. If I had known this, I am sure lots of my stress about finding a job would have been decreased."

"Do what you can, and it will work out. If you don't have the money, maybe that is God's way of telling you to go in a different direction."

ON YOUR WAY

Trust God from the bottom of your heart;
don't try to figure out everything on your own.
Listen for God's voice in everything you do, everywhere you go;
he's the one who will keep you on track.

PROVERBS 3:5-6

Life is full of endings and beginnings. Up to this point in your life, graduation may be one of the biggest. But there will be many others. Writing the conclusion to a book is like graduation. Something is finished; on to the next challenge, the next mountain. But it is good and right to savor the moment. Make it a few moments of unbridled euphoria. Celebrate in your own style—the arm pump; the bent-knees slide with a yell;

the jump-around; the throw-something-in-the-air-and-hope-it-doesn't-hurt-anybody release.

The people who have prepared you for graduation sincerely hope you'll remember everything they tried to teach you. They know that won't actually happen. They don't remember everything others tried to teach *them* along the way. At a deeper level, they hope you remember what's important—not that you remember everything you learned but how to learn and the joy of learning. We trust that even when the stories fade and the illustrations get dated, the truth of the Choice Matrix will remain to help guide your decisions. We don't expect you to remember all the specifics of what we told you, but we deeply hope that you remember being understood, cared for, encouraged, corrected, and inspired. Being on your way means being aware of those ahead of you and those behind you in life.

Ecclesiastes is the graduation book of the Bible. It was written by the wisest man to ever live to guide young people into a good life. God gave Solomon a lot of wisdom, and Solomon, the human being that he was, learned a lot of wisdom the way all of us do: the hard way. Ecclesiastes reads like the blog of a person who decided to test truth and life. He had the means to do it, so he did. And he discovered that without a continual acknowledgement of God, life turns into smoke and mirrors. The meaning in life always fades away if we leave God out.

Graduation includes a very special kind of remembering: deciding what you are going to keep in mind as you go along your way. Solomon's counsel has stood the test of time: "Honor and enjoy your Creator while you're still young" (Ecclesiastes

12:1). We already touched on Solomon's final entry to his blog, but it is worth concluding our time together with the same thoughts:

The last and final word is this:

> *Fear God.*
> *Do what he tells you.*

> *And that's it. Eventually God will bring every-thing that we do out into the open and judge it according to its hidden intent, whether it's good or evil. (verses 13-14)*

Congratulations! Well done. You're on your way. God goes with you.

More great titles from the NavPress TH1NK line!

A Grad's Guide to Time with God
TH1NK
978-1-60006-436-4

Devotional time has never been easier or better for grad students. Take seven minutes a day to build your faith, grow closer to God, and make progress in your spiritual life with ten weeks of creative daily devotions. Written for students by students, the devotions help you put your faith into practice through fasting, prayer, and worship. Start a new habit of looking to God first every day.

The Message//REMIX 2.0
Eugene H. Peterson
978-1-60006-002-1

The Message//REMIX redefines what it means to read God's Word. Now slimmer and with added features—including expanded intros, maps, topical index, and more—the *REMIX 2.0* is now even more versatile.

Memorize This
D. Mason Rutledge
978-1-57683-457-2

God's Word affects our day-to-day lives. The verses you memorize really change the way you live. The Scripture in this specialized version of NavPress's successful *Topical Memory System* can help teens and college students deal with whatever life throws at them.

To order copies, call NavPress at 1-800-366-7788 or
log on to www.navpress.com.